BIBLE VERSES

about

CONFIDENCE

A Daily Devotional to Overcome Anxiety

GRACE MCEWAN

CONTENTS

LIVING IN
ABSOLUTE POWER

~🙵~

Hello dear sisters, and welcome to 365 days of living in Absolute Power. No matter where you are in your journey of self-discovery, know this—God knew you, God knows you and He loves you…no matter what! I say this with such ease and confidence now, but there was a time when I doubted it—and therefore doubted myself.

I defined myself by the world's view and not by God's view. I looked at myself through the unappreciative eyes of a man who hadn't thought me valuable enough to be faithful to, and I simply thought that I could only find happiness if I changed, altered and "worked on" myself from the outside.

I didn't realise that I had to be transformed from within, in order to see myself as my Heavenly Father did. I couldn't bring myself to believe that everything the Creator creates is perfect, and therefore I am perfect too. I couldn't look at myself in the mirror without picking out a dozen or more flaws that I felt I needed "to work on" before I could feel better about myself.

It got really bad, because the moment I began to work on one set of flaws that I perceived through my unenlightened eyes, there unfolded a whole new set of defects that I felt I needed to work on. As the list of flaws grew longer, my self-confidence diminished to the point where I just couldn't feel good about myself at all.

It grew harder and harder for me and eventually, through the mists of a dark depression, I reached for my Bible in desperation, and read the words:

> *"I praise you, for I am fearfully and wonderfully made. Wonderful are your works; my soul knows it very well."*
>
> PSALM 139:14

I began to ponder on these words. I meditated on them… and my Heavenly Father reached into my heart and turned my eyes towards Him. He helped me see how He created us—each in His own image. There are no imperfections in Him. Therefore, I am perfect—just the way I am. And you are too, my sister. You are perfect—just the way you are.

So while you're muddling through this journey called life, take a moment to look in the mirror—not to adjust your makeup or pat your hair into place, but to adjust your view of yourself and pat yourself on the back, because every time you appreciate how God sees you, you move one step forward on your journey to self-acceptance and self-confidence.

I went on a journey from self-pity and self-condemnation to self-confidence and self-appreciation, and every day began with a simple study of one of God's promises from the scriptures. So I share this with you, and may you be blessed by the Power of your Heavenly Father's thoughts that rest on you every day.

Remember—you are fearfully and wonderfully made! His works are wonderful. And you are wonderful too!

GRACE MCEWAN

JANUARY

JANUARY 1

❦

She is clothed with strength and dignity.

PROVERBS 31:25

S o your make-up's running, those six inch heels are killing off your feet by the second, and maybe you should have been realistic, and not hoped that you would be comfortable in an 'S' when it's obvious you're an 'L'…and now you're wondering if your face is turning blue because you are too scared to breathe, lest you snap the waistband of those overly tight jeans.

The fact is, you are not seeing yourself as who you were meant to be, and you are trying to be someone you think you ought to be. You're not the only one trying to fit into a persona that they think is better than the one they were born with. The world is filled with women who aren't looking at the reality of who they are—not as their peers see them, but as God does. He has created you to be uniquely you—confident and proud of who you are—in Him. So step into something more comfortable—yourself in Christ! He is your Confidence!

JANUARY 2

Do not be discouraged for the
Lord your God is with you.

JOSHUA 1:9

The kitchen is a mess—pots and pans strewn all around; sauce on the walls where you slung some just because you were so frustrated at not getting it right. There's this lingering smell of cinders and you're devastated because they were the vegetables you were trying so hard to sauté to perfection just like the recipe said you were supposed to. And life's like that—you have a rosy view of it when you start out—that it's going to be like this perfect meal you were going to create to impress someone—with every dish worthy of an Instagram post. But now you're stuck with cleaning up the mess. Actually no—you don't have to do this alone. He is with you. The Creator of the Universe is with you. Jesus is with you. And He will deal with your mess and turn it into a Message. Because the recipe for success and confidence starts with Him!

JANUARY 3

~

I praise you because I am fearfully and wonderfully made.

PSALM 139:14

New Year—new weight loss plan and workout schedule. Well, that's what you started out with. A strained tendon and several aching muscles later, you're close to abandoning that ridiculously strenuous regimen for a reality check. Here's the deal. You can do this—just take it one step at a time, set no unrealistic goals and make the whole weight loss plan *doable*. God has designed you to be perfectly made—"fearfully and wonderfully made"! Confidence in His ability to help you find your way to the right end of the scales will help you reach those goals. Above all, realise your worth as a woman who has been blessed with the presence of God in her. Go on a diet of His Word to instil confidence in your abilities… and stand strong on the foundation of His Promises.

JANUARY 4

꧁

*Finally, be strong in the Lord
and in his mighty power.*

EPHESIANS 6:10

You can do this. You've got this. Yes, everybody's been telling you things that sound hollow. After all, there's a hole where your heart once was and it's going to take a while for the healing to take place. Or so you think. The fact is, you don't have to do this alone. And you don't have to rely on your own strength to get you through this time. It's hard…but He makes it easier—by giving you His strength. And suddenly—you're stronger. Strong enough to let go of that relationship that wasn't quite working any way. Strong enough to believe that you will love again. So… chin up lady. He's got this…and that's why you can do this!

JANUARY 5

I can do all things through
Him who strengthens me.

PHILIPPIANS 4:13

Sometimes it doesn't seem like it, does it? Not when the job you have feels like a marathon you can't run anymore…because the work you have pending has turned into the mountain you can't climb. You're probably feeling like a juggler who hasn't got it all together and, maybe, you're even doubting your skills as a multi-tasker. What you need to remember is that you are a woman and you are blessed with a natural ability to multitask. All you need to do is take a deep breath and remember that God created you with some pretty awesome gifts and talents. And when you tap into Him, you tap into all those abilities you forgot that you possessed. What's more, He cares about you. He gives you all the strength you need. With Him, in Him and through Him—you are a Confident Woman.

JANUARY 6

✥

Do not be anxious about anything, but in every situation, by prayer and petition, with thanksgiving, present your requests to God.

PHILIPPIANS 4:6

This might not come across as the ideal piece of advice if paying off a mortgage or a student loan is keeping you up at night… or if you're at crossroads and haven't the faintest idea how your career plans (or the lack of them) are going to pan out. These words might seem even harder to believe when you've cried yourself into oblivion over a recent heartbreak. Yet the simple truth is—***this is the only advice you will ever need*** to get through life while staying on an even keel, and even being a source of strength to the people around you.

Worry doesn't solve anything and only serves to quell your spirit. Take some quiet time by yourself and tap into that connection you have with your Heavenly Father. The fact is, your Daddy up in heaven loves His daughter so much and doesn't ever want to see her cry or be stressed about life. He just wants you to trust Him and to know that He will make it all better.

JANUARY 7

~

Do not be afraid; you will not be
put to shame. Do not fear disgrace;
you will not be humiliated.

ISAIAH 54:4

So you wake up every morning and feel like you're on a long ride down a dead end. Which basically means you've been dating someone who isn't looking like he's going to be popping the question and you've been waiting a long time for it. 'Speak now or forever hold your peace'. Well you thought you were going to hear those words at your wedding… and now you just know that you have to follow that instruction yourself. For your own peace of mind. You wanted to hold on but maybe it's time to let go. Bite the bullet before it explodes. It's kinder in the long run. So if you know that the person you're with isn't thinking long term and you are, rip the band aid off. Don't waste your time. Tell him what's on your mind. Be fearless. Above all, pray over the situation and know that God cares. He also knows what's best for you… and He will lead you to it.

JANUARY 8

❧

For the Spirit God gave us does not make us timid, but gives us power, love, and self-discipline.

2 TIMOTHY 1:7

Right—you feel like you made a mess of a situation. You thought you could be more in control, but you were afraid to speak up, speak out or just speak. Your voice somehow failed you, because suddenly you had no words. They were there—somewhere—but they didn't form or come out quite like you had hoped they would. Maybe you had even rehearsed in front of the mirror. This could have been an interview or a first date. And what was that about '*love*? You didn't feel it? It wasn't there? You didn't love the job you had to do? As for self-discipline—stop beating yourself up about what's done and move forward, girl—you're going to get more opportunities to do it all again, and this time like the champion you are! So pick up the promise of the power, love and self-discipline given to you by your Heavenly Father... and be strong!

JANUARY 9

Be on your guard; stand firm in the faith; be courageous; be strong.

1 CORINTHIANS 16:13

It's a fact. There are situations and people out there that you can't blindly trust. It's time to exercise your women's intuition. Just for a while, pretend you're a powerful, female Sherlock Holmes. Well, don't go social media stalking anybody, but probably take a discreet peek into the goings-on of whoever it is that's making you feel that there's more to them than meets the eye. And then, tackle the problem head on. Don't beat around the bush. Ask the person what they're up to without conducting a full-scale interrogation. Pray before you speak, and He will give you the words. Maybe it's a cheating partner, or maybe it's someone who's trying to steal your job from under your nose. You know you're a strong woman, right? Courageous too. Tap into those qualities and stand up for your rights. Your Heavenly Father wants the very best for you. He's looking out for you.

JANUARY 10

God is within her, she will not fall;
God will help her at break of day.

PSALM 46:5

You stumble out of bed and the first thing you need is a cup of coffee. But you've forgotten to stop at the grocery store and buy milk and you like your coffee white with sugar. You're not a morning person and the break of day isn't your favourite time. Neither is it your best time. So consider your frustration when you are caught at your worst. You are heaping recriminations upon yourself instead of stopping and really appreciating the beauty of a new day and the goodness of God who brought you safely through another night and set you on your feet—complete, whole and strong. So today, instead of your morning fix of coffee, reach for something stronger—the love of your Heavenly Father. Take a large sip of His word. Talk to Him about how you're feeling and watch Him transform your mood. You'll feel the '*Son*'shine warm your soul!

JANUARY 11

*But blessed is the one who trusts in
the Lord, whose confidence is in Him.*

JEREMIAH 17:7

"Okay," you say, "but aren't I supposed to trust in my-self? Aren't I supposed to have confidence in my own abilities? Isn't being a girl today all about being self-reliant and independent?"

I knew someone we shall call Tammy Spelling. Cheerleader, Homecoming Queen, Prom Queen. Everyone aspired to be like her, because everybody really liked her. She was also smart and went on to a great college career. Someone once asked Tammy her secret. She looked confused. "What secret?" she asked. "The secret of your great strength and confidence," was the reply.

She smiled bashfully and shrugged. "Oh, I'm the timidest person I know," she said, "and I'm not saying that to seem modest. I honestly am. But I gave my insecurities to Jesus… and ever since, I have begun the day looking in the mirror and seeing not me—but He who is the strength within me."

So when that expensive makeover hasn't worked, you're not feeling the new hairstyle and your make up has definitely made you look like someone you don't recognize, get to work on what lies within, and give it all to Him.

JANUARY 12

Be strong and courageous. Do not be afraid; do not be discouraged for the Lord your God is with you wherever you go.

JOSHUA 1:9

Franklin D. Roosevelt said, "Courage is not the absence of fear but the ability to act in spite of it." And you're probably thinking to yourself, 'Yes, I have the ability to act despite my fear—*I run*!' How many of us make that mistake and then miss out on the rewards of standing our ground and facing fear head on. Fear of failure is probably the worst… because it is largely based on how we perceive ourselves. And God is actually telling you not to worry because He is with you wherever you go. So even in the direst situation—and even when you're just trying to do the right thing in the face of all opposition, hold on to His promise. You stand your ground girl, and let people see what you're capable of—in Him.

JANUARY 13

～

She opens her mouth with wisdom, and
the teaching of kindness is on her tongue.

PROVERBS 31:26

Ah yes, this *'she'* is you. "But," you say, "*whenever I open my mouth, I generally put my foot in it!*" You're not alone in this. A lot of us frequently say the first thing that comes to mind and shoot our mouths off. Yet God is speaking these words through King Solomon who was known for his wisdom, and also for the number of women he had around him. You were created to speak wisdom; to show and teach kindness. Believe it and remember it—most especially when you are in the mood to speak anything but wisdom and show anything but kindness. Because it would be going against the very nature that you were given by your Creator. Remember it most especially when someone shows you disrespect and casts aspersions on your intelligence. Tell them who you really are!

JANUARY 14

❧

By the grace of God, I am what I am.

1 CORINTHIANS 15:10

You've been struggling to be accepted. You changed the colour of your hair, got a tan, splurged on a new wardrobe, and even learned a new sport that led to a couple of torn ligaments, simply because you are not made for strenuous physical activity. So now you're limping along—bone weary, your muscles aching, and your self-image at an all-time low. Cheer up, because what you are is '*fearfully and wonderfully made*'! Which doesn't mean that you scare people off, but rather that they look upon you with respect. It also doesn't mean that you are less than anyone else. Don't sell yourself short by calculating your worth by the length of your skirt or the depth of your neckline. Or by trying to change things about your physical appearance only because someone made a personal remark. Nobody's perfect, and that's a fact. Acceptance of who you are is acceptance of what you can be by His Grace.

JANUARY 15

❧

Trust in the Lord with all your heart,
and do not lean on your own understanding.
6 In all your ways acknowledge him,
and he will make straight your paths.

PROVERBS 3:5-6

Yes, the path so far has been convoluted and often crooked. You've tripped, fallen, hauled yourself up and now you're just feeling ragged. It's time for a reality check. You can't do life on your own. You've tried it and you've realized that the understanding of the world that you thought you had, was totally skewed—something like the path you were following. Here's the deal—when your thoughts or views are skewed, so is your path. You need to stop right here, right now, and recalibrate. It all begins with trusting in the Lord—with your emotions as well as your intellect. Because only when you give Him control of both, can He straighten out your thinking and, consequently, your path. You'll soon see things falling into place and your life choices and goals making better sense.

JANUARY 16

Blessed is she who believed that the
Lord would fulfil His promises to her.

LUKE 1:45

It's alright to admit to yourself that you have, over time, lost your faith in the promises of people. They make vows only to break them, and you're not just weary of this attitude, but are also on the fast track to lifelong cynicism. So basically, you are shying away from establishing deeper friendships and are definitely not in the market for yet another potentially failed relationship. Here's the truth, girl—your trust issues are creating a barrier between you and a lifetime of happiness. Here's what you need to do—tap into the promises that God made to you. Believe and claim them. They are the only reassurance you will ever need! This is how it works—if you trust God to come through on His promises, He will never disappoint you. What's more, when you trust God, He gives you the ability to repose that trust only in the people who will never disappoint you.

JANUARY 17

~⅃

For we are God's handiwork,
created in Christ Jesus...

EPHESIANS 2:10

When you stand back and admire that canvas you've just finished painting, the piece you've written, or anything that you've made from scratch with your own hands, you know what your Creator feels like when He looks at you. While you, on the other hand, probably take a look at your reflection in the mirror and feel more like a train wreck, than God's handiwork...on most days. When you do, try to step back and look at yourself through His eyes— how strong, courageous and beautiful He has created you to be. How much care and love He has poured into every tiny detail that makes you who you are. You are unique, and in Him you are the courageous woman He created you to be.

JANUARY 18

~

For I know the plans I have for you," declares the Lord, "plans to prosper you and not to harm you, plans to give you hope and a future.

So yes, it looks like everyone's life is going somewhere, while you're stuck in pretty much the same rut you have been in—and it doesn't matter how many wardrobe makeovers you've had, it still feels like you've been sleeping in the same clothes and waking up with messy hair and makeup every morning. It's a perception that you have of your life because you're probably looking at the people around you and wondering when your time will come. The fact is, your time is here. Your time is now. Just change your outlook. Alter your perception of your life and future. Because even if you feel like you don't have it together, He does. He has it all figured out for you. So hold your head up high and walk tall.

JANUARY 19

❧

May the God of hope fill you with
all joy and peace as you trust in him,
so that you may overflow with hope
by the power of the Holy Spirit.

ROMANS 15:13

It's incredible how other people seem so positive and upbeat. You've tried getting into their heads and emulating their lives, but it hasn't worked. You've only managed to pull a tendon—again—while trying out some new dance moves, and your cello lessons were abruptly halted when a neighbor complained. So where do you go from here? The thing is, there are some things that all the striving and effort in the world can never buy. These things are freely bestowed on you when you ask for them, without ever doubting that you will definitely receive them. One of them is joy—not the temporal earthly joy, but that which comes from above. The other is peace—that incredible gift that you are given in exchange for unquestioning trust in His plans for your life. So hey, it's time to claim these for yourself and begin to really live…in Him.

JANUARY 20

You are altogether beautiful, my darling; there is no flaw in you.

SONG OF SOLOMON 4:7

Surprising though this fact may seem to you, you don't need a nose job, and you definitely don't need to change anything at all about yourself. Because the amazing thing is— God doesn't want to change a thing about you. He loves you just the way you are. Because He created you and declared you beautiful and flawless. So even when it's that time of the month and your hormones are all over the place; you've broken out in spots and you feel less than perfect, remember that your Creator made all things perfect and flawless. So take a break from critically appraising your reflection in the mirror, and instead go out and enjoy being who you were meant to be. A self-assured, self-confident, courageous young woman who has the world at her feet.

JANUARY 21

～

*You will be a crown of splendor in
the Lord's hand, a royal diadem
in the hand of your God.*

Is. 62:3

If you're skeptical about your self-worth, recalling how God perceives you can give you an instant boost. Faith in His promises is the key to self-confidence. It doesn't matter what the world thinks. Remember that He thinks differently from the world, because He is God and He is above this world. Royalty is not earned, it is bestowed. It is in your DNA. The crazy thing is, you are a princess in His kingdom, and not just that, He also things of you as a 'crown of splendour' and a 'royal diadem'—which literally means, you are a jewel in His Kingdom. Wow! Hard to consider that thought when your confidence is ebbing…or perhaps now is the time to take pause and wear this truth like a royal robe of self-assurance.

JANUARY 22

❧

*No temptation has overtaken you that
is not common to man. God is faithful,
and he will not let you be tempted beyond
your ability, but with the temptation
he will also provide the way of escape,
that you may be able to endure it.*

1 CORINTHIANS 10:13

Now this is a powerful assurance. We all know how great temptation can be. Including the temptation to think of yourself as less than you actually are—which might lead you to allow people to use you, or even get into destructive relationships. Girl, you don't need to compromise your values and morals to be accepted, or fit in with the world's view of who or what you need to be. Temptation is all around. But you have the courage and strength to resist it—in Him.

JANUARY 23

～

*In the same way, the women are
to be worthy of respect.*

1 TIMOTHY 3:11

You may not be perfect. You may not think of yourself as the ideal woman. You may have made mistakes and even taken a few wrong turns in your life's journey so far, but you are worthy of respect. Each time you acknowledge your weakness and rely on God's strength, you are worthy of respect. Each time you fall and pick yourself up you are worthy of respect. Each time you choose to be less 'popular' because you have made the right choice, you are worthy of respect. You are worthy of respect because God said you are. After all you are his daughter!

JANUARY 24

Your workmanship is marvelous—
how well I know it.

PSALM 139:13-14

Rejection hurts. Acceptance reinforces. Yes, it's a fact for sure. Obviously you are one of a whole world of women who simply want to be accepted for who they are. But it's not that simple if you are going to look to the world for that validation. Look to God instead. He loves you even when your hair is messy, and he especially loves you when your mascara is running after you've had a good cry as you take the burdens of your insecurities to Him. You are his workmanship, after all, and He delights in you.

JANUARY 25

~

For we are God's handiwork, created in Christ Jesus.

EPHESIANS 2:10

As God's handiwork, you are more valuable than you may even be aware. Take the finest piece of art available on the planet and multiply that by infinity. That's how valuable you are to God, and that's how you need to see yourself—far more beautiful, strong and courageous than you give yourself credit for. Often you might find yourself so caught up in an endless process of trying to change your appearance to meet the shallow expectations of the world, that you miss out on the only reinforcement you need of your worth and value—the Word.

JANUARY 26

❧

Be strong and courageous. Do not be afraid or terrified because of them, for the Lord your God goes with you; he will never leave you nor forsake you.

DEUTERONOMY 31:6

It's heartening to know that God never left the building even when your best friend did. It's also encouraging to remember that He was, is, and will be, right by your side when you face ridicule or intimidation. It's hard when you feel like you don't fit in, or are being misunderstood. So next time your throat is dry and you can barely speak because fear has its fingers around your vocal chords, take a breath and draw courage from the fact that you are never alone in this battle. Your heavenly daddy has got this. So don't let anyone take your voice or your spirit away.

JANUARY 27

❧

And why do you worry about clothes?
See how the flowers of the field grow.
They do not labour or spin. Yet I tell
you that not even Solomon in all his
splendour was dressed like one of these.

MATTHEW 6:28-29

Sure, it's an important date. You want to look your best. Around you are strewn clothes that you have tried on and discarded, because somehow, nothing seems right. You think one dress is too unflattering, and the other too plain. One seems to say you are desperate and the other that you are too conservative. But girl, it isn't what you wear, but who you are within yourself, and God has created you perfectly. No matter what you wear, you will look beautiful, if you project the beauty that is within you. And you can only do that if you believe in it. Step outside for a moment and look at the flowers… and know that God dressed each of them himself—perfectly! He will do the same for you!

JANUARY 28

❦

*Who of you by worrying can add
a single hour to your life?*

LUKE 12:25

You're young, and though you have concerns and challenges, worrying is the last thing you should do. Worry destroys, defeats and deflates. You can wake up in the morning floating on cloud nine, and a single worrying thought can send you hurtling down to the depths of despair and gloom. There's really no point to worry, because it's counterproductive. So, stand on top of worry and stomp it down. Deflate, destroy it and defeat it before it does all of that to you. Choose to be positive and to say something self-affirming to yourself every day. You will feel calm and buoyant—and we know that tranquillity is the secret to confidence.

JANUARY 29

~

What, then, shall we say in response to these things? If God is for us, who can be against us?

ROMANS 8:31

It sure might seem like the world is against you. Everything seems to be going wrong. People keep telling you that you're at the threshold of life and you have the world at your feet, while you feel like the world has its feet all over you and is trampling you down. It's good to remember, at this point, that you have an indulgent Heavenly Father—one who knows exactly what you're going through, and He will make sure that things are set right. In the meantime, reinforce your courage with the certain truth that He is in your corner and nobody can mess with you because He simply won't allow it!

JANUARY 30

❧

And I am convinced that nothing can
ever separate us from God's love.

ROMANS 8:38

There's something about love. It can really make you feel like you have wings and can fly! But almost always, you have to float back to the ground like a balloon that is rapidly losing air, and you might even wonder—was that even love? There is, however, one love that never fails. It is the love that your Creator has for you. It lifts you up and sets you on your feet. It gives you all the validation you need, and it renews your confidence and courage. The best part about this love is that it never goes away. Nor can anyone take it away from you. Nothing can tear you apart from this love. This love is all you need in order to live the life of a strong, competent, confident woman.

JANUARY 31

❧

In all these things we are more than conquerors through him who loved us.

ROMANS 8:37

Look at you! You made it to the end of the first month of the year and you're looking g-o-o-d! You have power surging through your veins. You have renewed strength and confidence as you lean into the abundance that God provides for His little girl. You're loved, cared for and sometimes even corrected—just so you get it right the next time around. He's a dad after all. He's got a treat lined up for you today, because you've done a great job this whole month. He's giving you a perfect day, and even if you look up and see a cloud, it has a silver lining. So step outside and take a deep breath. What you smell all around you is success, challenges overcome, and valuable lessons learned. It's the most fragrant bouquet ever! And it emanates from the confidence that you have discovered within yourself. You are a conqueror, so get ready to take on the world!

NOTES

FEBRUARY

FEBRUARY 1

❧

See what great love the Father has lavished
on us, that we should be called children
of God! And that is what we are!

1 JOHN 3:1

Well, it's not often you consider this truth—that you are a child of God. And if a child of God, then a privileged citizen of the world. How come then, you say, you so often feel so unlike all the things you're supposed to be? Well, put it down to a momentary—or sometimes chronic—lack of understanding of everything you can be through Christ who strengthens you. Woman, you're not weak, even though the world might sometimes lead you to think you are. You have an innate strength that comes to the fore whenever you call upon it. It's what God your father has gifted to you—lavished upon you—as his precious daughter. His love is your power, so draw upon it!

FEBRUARY 2

❧

Dear friends, let us love one another, for love comes from God. Everyone who loves has been born of God and knows God.

1 JOHN 4:7

Not taking that call from someone new you've just met. Refusing that invitation to join in an evening of wholesome fun. Choosing to keep to yourself rather than getting to know more of your peers, often indicates your own mistrust of love, and an inability to allow people into your life. The fact is, if you find it difficult to make friends, or hold on to relationships—both platonic and romantic—ponder on your understanding of God. Think about the natural bond you have with Him—your heavenly father. It gives you strength and confidence, and above all, it helps you to open your heart to people. Frankly, it will also catapult you to the top of the popularity charts!

FEBRUARY 3

We love because he first loved us.

1 JOHN 4:19

You're having a tough time because you are finding it difficult to love the people around you. It could be that you're in a new school or a new job—and somehow you are being excluded from those conversations around the coffee machine. It isn't the end of the world, and you don't need to judge yourself or feel like you're the villain here. You're just dealing with some issues based on your comprehension of love. Rule number one—don't overthink your inability to love certain people. Instead, just focus on love itself, as manifest in the person of your heavenly daddy. Once you allow yourself to be submerged in that unconditional love, you will find it a whole lot easier to love and accept others—while being loved and accepted yourself.

FEBRUARY 4

✧

Above all, love each other deeply, because love covers over a multitude of sins.

Simply put—love is blind. So, if you're wondering if your long term love interest is the one, here's a way to find out. If you're constantly looking for flaws and complaining about them to your bestie, and yet keep telling yourself that you are in love, then maybe it's time for a reality check. Because love really does blind you to what others may perceive as flaws, but to you may just seem the very adorable character traits of the one you are besotted with. Strong women make courageous choices, and if you want to live and operate in strength, it's time to assess your long term relationships so that you are making the most of life and allowing others to do the same.

FEBRUARY 5

⌑

*People look at the outward appearance, but
the Lord looks at the heart.*

1 SAMUEL 16:7

I heard this crazy story of a couple who were divorced on
their wedding night. The reason? For the first time ever,
the guy saw his woman without her fake hair, eyelashes and
makeup—which by all accounts she didn't go without, all
the while that they were dating. Silly girl, you say—why did
she decide to divest herself of them on her wedding night
of all things? Maybe she wanted a moment of honesty with
her husband. Maybe she loved him so much that she wanted
him to love her and she therefore did whatever she could
to win his heart—or his very shallow feelings. Here's what
you need to know—when a bunch of men were quizzed
on whether they thought girls looked more beautiful with
makeup on, most of the men said they preferred their women
without too much face paint. The men seeking committed
relationships said they were looking for woman who were
"natural". Today, get in touch with who you are. Take off
your painted face and test the waters without it. Let the love
in your heart set your face aglow!

FEBRUARY 6

❧

*Don't let anyone look down on you because
you are young, but set an example for
the believers in speech, in conduct,
in love, in faith and in purity.*

1 TIMOTHY 4:12

If someone hinted that you are young and naïve, set the record straight. Tell them that you may be young, but you are decisive, strong, courageous and intelligent. And then go ahead and encourage other young people around you to do likewise. The point is, you're taking over the world—and it's your turn to shine. You have been blessed with an intellect and access to information and skills that weren't accessible to the previous generation. Use them to your advantage. It's time to debunk the myth that young people are wild, immature and pleasure-seeking. Introduce everyone to the responsible, self-assured, focused and goal-oriented person you are. And while you're at it, take the hands of a few other young people around you and encourage them on their journey.

FEBRUARY 7

✥

Therefore, if anyone is in Christ, he is a new creation. The old has passed away; behold, the new has come.

2 CORINTHIANS 5:17

Are you feeling like you've run around in circles and tied yourself in knots in the process, and all you need is a fresh start? Have you tried to start over and keep looking back at all the mistakes you've made? Well, the good news is, you can get a complete makeover. All you need to do is submit to being changed and transformed as you surrender to Jesus. He will make you feel brand new. There's no better way to start over than with Him. You don't have to look back or feel any remorse or regret either. He just wipes the slate clean, and hands you the key to the future where you're stronger, more capable, and filled with fresh resolve.

FEBRUARY 8

❧

Be completely humble and gentle; be
patient, bearing with one another in love.

EPHESIANS 4:2

Yeah, I know, you don't feel particularly inclined to be either humble or gentle, let alone patient with a lot of people. The thing is, you don't want to be bogged down by unforgiveness or ill will. You want to be on top of it all. You want to be the bigger person. Here's a fact—the truly great are truly humble. So cast off your pride and draw upon that inherent humility and patience that defines you as a woman. Sometimes to be truly strong you also have to be truly gentle and loving. Do you want to be a conqueror? Then wield the arrows of love!

FEBRUARY 9

❧

After all, no one ever hated their own body, but they feed and care for their body, just as Christ does the church.

EPHESIANS 5:29

If you're someone who is struggling with image issues that are in turn causing you to neglect feeding and caring for your body, this is for you. Eating disorders stem from insecurity over your self-image. Social media does little to help, because everywhere you see women with unrealistically sculpted bodies. A negative, uninformed approach towards achieving such a perfect shape, might only result in harming both your mental and physical wellbeing. There's no harm in pursuing a healthier, fitter body, but do it intelligently. Above all, don't punish your body, but nurture it and feed it with health-promoting food…and exercise regularly. Be kind to your body and love it. Thank God for it every day.

FEBRUARY 10

~❧~

The life I now live in the body, I live by faith in the Son of God, who loved me and gave himself for me.

GALATIANS 2:20

You might not have all the answers right now, and you may not feel like you're doing what's best for you all the time. The answer lies in simple faith in your father God who created you and then made plans for your life. Allowing yourself to live in that faith brings strength, peace and courage, even when times are rough. Allowing yourself to live in that faith is permitting yourself to see yourself and your future as He sees it—defined by His grace and illuminated by his boundless love. Dear beautiful woman, dwell in this truth—He loved you so much that He gave Himself for you—transforming your life and future once and for all.

FEBRUARY 11

❧

*As the Father has loved me, so have I
loved you. Now remain in my love.*

JOHN 15:9

This love is like an umbrella. Step out of its protection, and you're exposed to the elements. It can get messy and isn't the best thing for your image. Remaining under the umbrella is the wisest thing you can do, because you can then enjoy life, hope…and love. The best part of being under this umbrella is that you will encounter others who draw from the same source of love that you do. You can form relationships and bonds based on trust and a shared faith in the completeness of that umbrella of protection. It's warm there. It's safe and secure. Today, open yourself to the experience of His love. Step beneath the umbrella and let His love envelope you!

FEBRUARY 12

❧

Do nothing out of selfish ambition
or vain conceit. Rather, in humility
value others above yourselves.

PHILIPPIANS 2:3

Well, you're constantly being told to be self-confident, so much so that humility seems to be in direct contrast to this directive. One thing that will define you as a woman of strength and dignity, is the manner in which you carry yourself. Where you're not constantly demanding your own way or trying to get ahead to meet your own goals at the expense of others…but rather that you wield that quiet confidence that respects and elevates those around you. Humility isn't being a doormat. It is acknowledging that others have a point of view too. Giving credence to others will enhance rather than diminish you in the eyes of the world.

FEBRUARY 13

❦

Before a downfall the heart is haughty,
but humility comes before honour.

PROVERBS 18:12

Whoa! There's that word again! H-u-m-i-l-i-t-y. What's with this word and why does it keep popping up over and over? The fact is, a little humility earns you rich dividends of R-e-s-p-e-c-t. So rather than throwing your weight about in school or at your job, let your goodness shine through. Quietly. As you help others to meet their goals and as you give everyone a chance to shine. The ability to lead others to greatness is the mark of a truly great leader. And you're a leader because you are God's child and He has placed responsibility upon your shoulders. So honey, step out today with a purpose. The purpose not to flaunt who you are but to humbly flow into the persona of who you were meant to be.

FEBRUARY 14

❧

Give thanks to the Lord, for he is good;
his love endures forever.

1 CHRONICLES 16:34

Amidst the chocolate coated hearts and bouquets of flowers; scented candles and intimate dinners for two, take some time to ponder the greatest love of all. The most enduring love. The love that gives and keeps giving. Today, seek that love. Seek it when you're feeling down about not having a Valentine's Day date. Seek it when you hear a song that reminds you of someone who said they'd love you forever and then let you down. Seek it when you're on the couch eating take out and watching television. It's the only love that will stand the test of time. It's His love. And when you have that love, you will attract people to you like moths to a flame. Because His love fills you with a certain confidence that no man can resist.

FEBRUARY 15

～

*Love must be sincere. Hate what
is evil; cling to what is good.*

ROMANS 12:9

Toss those books on dating advice out of the window and open the door to something real. It's called *sincere love*. It's the kind that cannot be learned or acquired. It is bestowed upon you. It comes when you wake up early in the morning and thank God for the gift of being alive. It falls gently upon your shoulders when you decide to visit someone who is feeling down. It floats around you like a golden cloud when you are so bone weary but decide to use your last vestiges of energy to help someone out. It fills you with unbounded joy and peace that never leaves, even when you are surrounded by life's inevitable storms. This is love that gives. Love that cares. Love that shares. It's the love every strong woman is capable of. Find it in yourself today!

FEBRUARY 16

❧

*See, I have engraved you on
the palms of my hands.*

ISAIAH 49:16

It's true, girl, you're really special. Not because the world decided that you are, but because God ordained it so. You are so special, in fact, that He has you literally engraved upon the palms of His hands. Those palms where the nails went through when He gave His life to make yours better. So if you're not feeling good about yourself, it's time to remind yourself that you ought to be. Let go of all that negativity that you've been wearing like a coat of armour. It's really like a repellent. Instead, let positivity shower its brilliance upon you. Wear confidence like a tiara. You are favoured. You are beautiful and people want to know you because they are aware of how special you are.

FEBRUARY 17

ꙅ

Since you are precious and honored in
my sight, and because I love you, I
will give people in exchange for you,
nations in exchange for your life.

ISAIAH 43:4

You never have to worry, even when it seems like your world, and you, are falling to pieces. You wanted things to work out one way and they didn't. It's alright. This isn't the end of the world, girl. So turn the music up and dance—even if it's only to drown out the sound of your own tears or cries of remorse. Because even when it seems like heaven's doors are closed, they are, in fact, opening a different way, and there's an army marching out to fight this battle on your behalf. Hey, you're never alone. Your big daddy who created this world and made you, has got this. He loves you and love, as you know, always finds a way. Today is going to be great, so put your game face on and get out there with a big smile. You're a winner and nothing can keep you down!

FEBRUARY 18

❧

What no eye has seen, what no ear has heard, and what no human mind has conceived—the things God has prepared for those who love him.

1 CORINTHIANS 2:9

You've set goals and objectives. You've made plans. Great. Now stop stressing about them. Relax. Take a deep breath and let it go. Begin to enjoy what you're doing. Live in the moment. Savour your pockets of downtime. Express yourself. Draw or paint. Visit your parents. Talk about something other than your future. Yes, we know that at this stage of your life that is paramount. It occupies pretty much all your thoughts and is the topic of every conversation. But you don't need to overthink the future quite so much. You've done your bit. You've stuck to your academic path. You've listened to your intuition. Your strength now lies in acknowledging that there's a Higher Power that has worked ceaselessly to bring you to this point—and that all the worrying in the world cannot influence what lies beyond. The fact is, He has a plan... and His plans are far more amazing than yours ever could be.

FEBRUARY 19

❧

*See what great love the Father has lavished
on us, that we should be called children
of God! And that is what we are!*

1 JOHN 3:1

It's not uncommon to feel unloved sometimes. It's even quite common for some people to feel unloved a lot of the time. This world with all its many challenges and distractions has made everyone so busy, that it's difficult for people to even find time to express their love for their…umm…loved ones! It's quite ironic, actually. So you aren't alone. There are others out there feeling like you are at the moment. The good part is that love falls like rain from heaven, submerging everyone whose hearts are open to it. Receive it… and then let it flow through you and fall on someone else who desperately needs it. You are a daughter of God—with a heart that reflects His love. You are a child of heaven itself, highly favoured, loved and cherished. Remind yourself of this fact the next time you feel unloved.

FEBRUARY 20

✦

Let love and faithfulness never leave you;
bind them around your neck, write
them on the tablet of your heart. Then
you will win favour and a good name
in the sight of God and man.

PROVERBS 3:3-4

Ah 'Favour'! Who doesn't crave it? And doesn't every strong courageous woman have it? Is it earned or is it freely available? So many questions! Actually, favour is bestowed when you least expect it, and when you are not seeking it. It comes when you don't even think you deserve it. It can come when you're waiting tables and feeling like a wreck…and you get the biggest tip you ever got. It can come when you're crawling out of bed early in the morning after a particularly tough previous day…when a friend picks you up and brings you breakfast. And it can come when you're feeling undeserving and God drops a bonus into your lap— simply because He loves you and has watched you quietly struggle and not quit. Favour comes as you unswervingly stay the course and keep going.

FEBRUARY 21

❧

*Know therefore that the Lord your God
is God; he is the faithful God, keeping
his covenant of love to a thousand
generations of those who love him
and keep his commandments.*

DEUTERONOMY 7:9

There's something so unique about a woman. Every woman. You have poise and grace. You have the ability to nurture and care for people. You feel sympathy and empathise with people. You have a heart overflowing with love. You can cry with those who weep and dry someone's tears with a simple word of hope and comfort. You are loyal to a fault and always stand up for those who you believe in. That's because you were created to reflect God's heart and love for people. If you feel less than capable of these qualities, then you need to step into who you really are today. This is not just an assumed persona—it's your character, etched and defined by your Creator. It's who you are, and who you were meant to be.

FEBRUARY 22

I have loved you with an everlasting love;
I have drawn you with unfailing kindness.

JEREMIAH 31:3

Being loved with an everlasting love places you in a position of significance. It reinforces the fact that you are important. Your role in this life is crucial and not to be taken lightly. Being shown unfailing kindness is to enjoy God's endless grace. It's to know that every moment is a fresh start and you don't need to haul any baggage around. You are travelling light. No stuff from the past impedes your progress. Your relationships improve because you are now confident in yourself and in who you are. You are not afraid—because of that confidence. Nor are you willing to compromise what you believe in. You don't let people take undue advantage of you. You gently but firmly make yourself heard. You are defined by your uniqueness.

FEBRUARY 23

❧

There is no fear in love. But
perfect love drives out fear…

1 JOHN 4:18

Yes, Perfect Love puts fear to flight. Fear of rejection. Fear of humiliation. Fear of the unknown. Fear of the future. Opening your heart to Love unlocks courage and bravery. Allowing yourself to feel that heavenly Love pour into you, is the key to discovering your inner strength and mettle. Woman, you have been given a promise. That you are loved with an everlasting love. Even when your hormones are acting up and you're blowing up or breaking down. The secret to riding out those storms is to remember that you are loved—and that you were created to be lovable.

FEBRUARY 24

❧

The Lord your God is with you,
the Mighty Warrior who saves.
He will take great delight in you.

ZEPHANIAH 3:17

Dear Princess, I know you've been dreaming of your Prince—the one who rides up on a white horse and rescues you from whatever horrible situation you have found yourself in. Perhaps you often sit alone in a corner of the Cafeteria and fantasize about him. Maybe you even shared the fantasy with a friend. Of course, people laughed because this is the stuff of fairy tales, isn't it? But strangely enough it can happen for you. Your Knight in Shining Armour is the Mighty Warrior who saves. This is your Prince of Peace who dries your tears when you cry… and fills your heart with His comforting presence when you're feeling alone and rejected. Even if nobody else seems to enjoy your company, He does. In fact, He *delights* in you! Best of all, He makes you stronger. The more time you spend with Him, the more capable you become to handle just about anything.

FEBRUARY 25

～

You, my brothers and sisters, were
called to be free. But do not use your
freedom to indulge the flesh.

GALATIANS 5:13

Love sets you free. Free to be the woman you were meant to be. Revel and rejoice in this freedom. But even as you are dancing in the rain, remember that your state of freedom is attractive to people around you and it's important to operate within some boundaries. Because even freedom needs a fence—sometimes…or you open yourself to intruders that seek only to destroy your newfound happiness. The spirit is willing but the flesh is weak, you might say, but understand how important it is to exercise caution when it comes to things of the flesh. Freedom is prudence that protects your heart and shields you from pain.

FEBRUARY 26

∾

In his love he will no longer rebuke you,
but will rejoice over you with singing.

ZEPHANIAH 3:17

Okay so you goofed up. You did something you can't forgive yourself for and maybe you think that the wrath of heaven is about to devour you. Stop the self-recrimination because it's crippling, and you need to get on with life. Your demanding academic schedule cries out for attention, and you can't afford to be wallowing in self-blame when you have so many important deadlines to meet. Remember that your heavenly daddy is waiting for you—eager to pick you up when you fall, heal the wounds and forgive you for not listening to him in the first place, when He warned you of danger. It's ok. You took a wrong turn and suffered the consequences, but there is no wrath coming down on you—only love!

FEBRUARY 27

⁓

But the fruit of the Spirit is love, joy, peace, forbearance, kindness, goodness, faithfulness, gentleness and self-control.

GALATIANS 5:22-23

Well, that's the fruit of the Spirit. The 'fruits' of 'spirits', on the other hand, are quite the opposite. And if it feels like peer pressure is drawing you towards indulging in more than the occasional drink, maybe it's time to stop and assess your situation. Girl, you were meant to be strong from within yourself… and sadly alcohol brings you down rather than builds you up. Don't be fooled—it slowly eats away at your ability to reason and distinguish between what's right and what isn't. It blurs your vision and frees your tongue in a not so great way. To reinforce your strength as a woman, seek to display the fruits of the Spirit. They are all the beautiful traits that define your nature as the woman of worth that you are. Have a beautiful day sunshine!

FEBRUARY 28

Let his banner over me be love.

SONG OF SONGS 2:4

Love is multi-dimensional. It is gentle when it comforts and fierce when it protects. It's like a river in spate when it flows unfettered, and the dew on the grass each morning when it drops almost silently upon you. Woman— you are love in all its many dimensions. You are beautiful, perfect, indefinable, extraordinary love. You make families and relationships complete. Your role is significant. Don't doubt your sphere of influence. People are looking up to you. People are eager to hear your point of view. Your opinion counts. Speak out fearlessly. Stand up for what you believe to be right. You are never too young to be who you were meant to be—a strong courageous woman.

NOTES

MARCH

MARCH 1

❧

*Come to me, all you who are weary and
burdened, and I will give you rest.*

MATTHEW 11:28

Going on a long trek takes you through the highs
and lows of the beautifully diverse countryside. The
landscape sometimes dips into the hollow of a serene blue
lake and walking along the banks can elevate your mood
like nothing else can. The tranquility of the lake restores and
recharges. You might stop awhile and just gaze out across
the water and watch birds dive for fish. Life is like a long
trek. The lake is Him who supplies your every need. When
He invites you to rest in Him, it's okay to leave your busy
schedule for a little while and chill out in the presence of the
Giver of all Life. It's strengthening and nourishing, and you
need it in order to come into your own as a strong, confident,
courageous woman.

MARCH 2

❧

*And I am sure of this, that he who
began a good work in you will bring it to
completion at the day of Jesus Christ.*

PHILIPPIANS 1:6

It's good to know that you're a work in progress. We all are. This means that there can be revisions and rewrites. It means that there's always something to look forward to— some new twist or turn in your narrative that will mould and shape you to be the woman you are meant to be. Being a work in progress also means that there is room for improvement. It means that you can build on your strengths and work on your weaknesses. And you don't have to do all the work. You are the work. He is building you up, and your story is constantly unfolding. It's pretty awesome. You are evolving constantly. And the future is beyond anything you could have imagined, so keep going!

MARCH 3

❧

*Truly I tell you, if anyone says to this
mountain, 'Go, throw yourself into the
sea,' and does not doubt in their heart
but believes that what they say will
happen, it will be done for them.*

MARK 11:23

Yes, you don't always begin the day feeling positive and there are some days when you don't want to get up at all. It's all a matter of having faith in your ability to move mountains—in and through Him. It could be a mountain of homework or a mountain of housework. It could be the mountain that has been growing between you and the man in your life, and you can't find the words to tell him that you don't feel the same way anymore…or that you feel your relationship needs some work. Whatever the mountain, know that you can move it—if you have faith in the ability of The One to whom all things are possible. Stay positive. And keep your faith alive!

MARCH 4

❧

You will keep in perfect peace
those whose minds are steadfast,
because they trust in you.

ISAIAH 26:3

Remember that time when you wanted to live that scene in a movie and took a flying leap into your boyfriend's arms? He was supposed to catch you by the waist and hold you aloft, but you came flying at him with such speed that he stepped back… and you will never live down the extreme humiliation of that moment. It's like leaning on a pillar that you thought was made of stone, only to discover it was a stage prop made from Styrofoam, and you landed in a heap on the floor, red faced and embarrassed. Isn't it great that there's a great big wonderful, awesome God that you can trust never to let you go and never to let you down? You can lean on Him anytime and He holds you up. You can run into His arms for comfort and He will uplift you. He never lets you down because He knows you are trusting in Him.

MARCH 5

❧

Follow God's example, therefore,
as dearly loved children.

EPHESIANS 5:1

There's a lesson that everyone learns in life, and that's the lesson about forgiveness. So many of us find it hard to let go of the wrongs that people have done to us. There are people who carry about that hurt all the time, so much so that they are limping from the exertion of bearing all that weight. Often you might not think that the people who hurt you deserve your forgiveness or your understanding. And then you are reminded of our forgiving, loving heavenly father. He never holds back on forgiveness. He wipes the slate clean each time you admit that you goofed up. He never reminds you of how many times He had to forgive you for the same mistake. He just lovingly welcomes you back into the peace that comes from being forgiven. Maybe today is the day that you extend that favour to someone you haven't been able to forgive. You'll walk lighter once you've shed that load of unforgiveness, believe me!

MARCH 6

This is the confidence we have in approaching God: that if we ask anything according to his will, he hears us.

1 JOHN 5:14

Remember that friend you had who kept praying that the cutest guy in the football team would fall in love with her and, when he didn't, she decided that she didn't believe in God and stopped praying? You know what the problem was, right? She wasn't asking for something that was in line with God's will. God probably had someone better for her further down the line and needed for her to focus on her school work right then. Well, she probably realised that later and went back to praying and believing. What are you praying for today? Perhaps you should stop and think about how long you have been saying that same prayer and why it isn't being answered. Sometimes you may have to wait…and at other times you may have to let go. Which do you think you need to do for your peace of mind?

MARCH 7

~

*With us is the Lord our God to
help us and to fight our battles.*

2 CHRONICLES 32:8

Beside every strong woman is a stronger, very reliable support system. Remember that time your mom went ahead of you on the way to school, to have a chat with that boy who was bullying you? Do you recall how at first you didn't want her to do that because it might make the other kids laugh at you, but after she had said her piece, people treated you right? That was the moment you felt a weight leave your tiny shoulders. Well, today your heavenly daddy wants to do the same for you. He wants to fight your battle on your behalf. He wants to go ahead of you and prepare the way so you can be safe. Are you ready to give him control and let him help you? Are you ready to discover how much stronger you are when you have Him on your side?

MARCH 8

~e

In him and through faith in him we may
approach God with freedom and confidence.

EPHESIANS 3:12

You always knew how to get your dad to bend the rules
a bit. It was to send in your mum with the request. You
knew she always managed to say the right words…because
she knew your dad so well. And also because he couldn't say
no to her. But that was a while ago when you were a little girl.
Now, evolving into the strong woman that you are, it seems
silly to expect someone else to do the asking on your behalf.
Yet there are times when you might not have the right words
to get your request across the table, and you desperately need
an answer to a problem. Like now, when you are faced with
an impossible task and don't know how to begin to tackle
it. But you have an 'advocate'—Jesus, to take your cares and
queries and present them to God. All you need is faith to
say the prayer.

MARCH 9

~

*Let us then approach God's throne
of grace with confidence, so that we
may receive mercy and find grace
to help us in our time of need.*

HEBREWS 4:16

Grace and confidence are two words which define a woman of faith, strength and courage. You might not feel that you are displaying either of these two qualities right now, because you aren't sure you even possess them. Grace comes from God. Confidence comes from faith in Him. Make them your two best friends and have them in your team at all times. You will win every time! Grace is having the humility to acknowledge that you can't do everything on your own. Confidence is the certainty that you can do just about anything with, in and through Him who gives you Grace. Wow lady, you are unstoppable when you have this figured out. Because you can take these two constant companions and approach God for help in your time of need and He will deliver you.

MARCH 10

❧

*The fruit of that righteousness will
be peace; its effect will be quietness
and confidence forever.*

ISAIAH 32:17

I magine that you are wandering through a vineyard, looking at the grapes ripening on the vines, and feeling the sun on your skin. It's a moment that you will never forget because you are feeling something you have never felt before in quite the same way and with quite the same intensity. It is peace, the fruit of righteousness. But you haven't quite figured out what righteousness is. It sounds kind of a hard thing to live up to, or be. It is. But when you are finding your way to God, and when you are intentionally seeking Him more and more, you discover His righteousness. He who can never do anything wrong then begins to work within you who seemingly always gets it wrong…and you are transformed. You become more confident in who you are—because who you are is who He has created you to be!

MARCH 11

❧

But blessed is the one who trusts in
the Lord, whose confidence is in him.

JEREMIAH 17:7

Ever watched the tide come in? Or the moon rise? Or the dawn break? Nature is so ordered. So well planned. If you spend enough time in the great outdoors, you will learn to gauge the moods and nuances of every shift in the wind and each cloud in the sky. You become one with it. It becomes a part of you. Trusting in a Higher Power and placing your confidence in the unseen is like that. The more time you spend listening to that soft voice, the more you will hear it. The more you take your prayers and requests to Him, the more answers you will receive. Your confidence in Him grows as His presence becomes a part of who you are. It's like standing in the path of a wave and watching it grow and grow…until it submerges you. You become one with it. It becomes a part of you. With it you are stronger. Apart from it you are bereft.

MARCH 12

❧

For the Lord will be at your side
and will keep your foot from being snared.

PROVERBS 3:26

You probably remember the times you tripped. You didn't see that object right there on the floor, or the bump on the ground, and you were in such a hurry that you just…tripped. No, it's not funny when you're trying so hard to look and feel graceful, and your limbs are all askew in that one embarrassing moment. So, you decide that you will be more careful next time, only you fail to slow down soon enough. Life's like that. Mistakes happen when you're not paying attention and don't swerve just in time to avoid the bump in the road. Wouldn't it be great if you had someone to keep a lookout on your behalf? Well, as it happens, you do. He is the Lord of Heaven's armies and He still thinks that you are important enough to have Him watch over you. He stays by your side so that you don't ever walk into a trap or get your toe stubbed. Because He cares about giving you the confidence you need to keep going.

MARCH 13

❧

For the Lord... takes the upright
into his confidence.

PROVERBS 3:32

Clinging to the sheer rock face on a steep ascent, you're wondering if you will make it to the top. It's been a hard climb, and there were moments when you thought your feet couldn't hold on any longer and your hands were weakening. But you kept going because you didn't want to seem like a quitter. Or maybe God whispered a truth in your ear. That you didn't have to put in any more effort, because He stepped in, the moment He saw that your striving was genuine. He wanted to help when He saw that you were committed to succeeding. He wouldn't let your feet slip and He kept your hands clinging on, because His nature is to support and encourage you when you are making an honest effort. He even shared His secrets of success with you. Because you tried, He helped you succeed.

MARCH 14

*Some trust in chariots and some
in horses, but we trust in the
name of the Lord our God.*

PSALM 20:7

It's important not to limit yourself to the temporal, but to place your trust in the eternal. The plans you lay have a fence around them, but the future He has planned for you is without boundaries. You can do pretty much anything when you have placed your trust in the Lord of the Universe. Chariots lose their wheels and horses their shoes, but God moves with the speed of lightning and like the rush of a summer breeze transforms everything. You don't have to drive your plans. God sets them fluidly in motion. You don't have to stress about your future. Even as we speak it is falling into place. That's why he tells you not to lay up treasures on this earth but to seek the Kingdom because it is the only place where you will be fulfilled.

MARCH 15

Our competence comes from God.

2 CORINTHIANS 3:4

Well, that doesn't mean that you're going to become an opera singer overnight or learn to tango like you've been doing it all your life. You have certain talents and skills that are your own. They have been given to you to use, develop and excel in. You know they are God-given, because when you exercise those skills and talents, you do it in a unique, seamless manner. This is the competence that He bestows on you. The ability to write, paint or sew. The ability to play an instrument, or even to plan and strategize. Discover your particular gift today and work on enhancing it with His help. He is the giver of every good gift and He is also the enhancer of ever good and perfect gift. The more you use it, the better it becomes. Think about your gifts and talents today. Don't bury them. Multiply them!

MARCH 16

~

*For the Spirit God gave us does
not make us timid, but gives us
power, love, and self-discipline.*

2 TIMOTHY 1:7

So your best friend asked you how she looked in her new hot pink dress with the slit up the side, and you told her exactly what you thought. Needless to say, she was upset. But you just wanted her to know that she looked like something she shouldn't look like…and using a word she didn't want to hear reduced her to tears. You made things worse by driving the point home, and she said she never wanted to speak to you again. So you're introspecting and thinking—have you been too outspoken? Do you feel like you can sometimes be overly aggressive or argumentative? Channel it. Or rather, ask God to help you use this quality effectively. The fact is, the world needs people like you—willing to tell it like it is. But you need to know how, when, and where. Temper your opinions with love. Deliver them with grace. You don't need to be timid and cover up the truth under a honeyed coat of destructive lies. Speak up and speak out the way God would do—forcefully, yet with love.

MARCH 17

❧

*So do not throw away your
confidence; it will be richly rewarded.
You need to persevere so that when
you have done the will of God, you
will receive what he has promised.*

HEBREWS 10:35-36

You set out to do something and you were super confident you would be a huge success. You didn't make a mess of things entirely, but you just didn't get where you hoped you would. Maybe it was a school project. Perhaps it was something for the community. The fact that you took a step in the right direction in the first place is commendable. But maybe your lack of success was because you didn't give yourself enough time to succeed. You were in too much of a hurry. God works in you through every experience—so you always come away learning something. Don't give up even when you think you're failing, because that's when you are about to have a breakthrough. Perseverance brings rich rewards.

MARCH 18

◦❧

Blessed is the one who perseveres under trial because, having stood the test, that person will receive the crown of life that the Lord has promised to those who love him.

JAMES 1:12

Do you ever wish you didn't have to face exams all the time? Do you ever dream of a time when schools will just do away with the whole process of assessment? Hmm… can gold be refined unless it passes through fire? When you go to visit a doctor, don't you trust him or her because they have passed a qualifying exam? When you trust yourself to a diving instructor, isn't it based on the fact that he or she has been trained for their job? Why then do you resist trials and challenges in life? The better thing would be to flow with them. Get on top of that challenge because you were made to be resilient. God shaped you to be a strong woman whose strength is in Him. Always remember that at the end of every exam is a certificate that says you are qualified!

MARCH 19

❧

*So we say with confidence, 'The Lord
is my helper; I will not be afraid.
What can mere mortals do to me?'*

HEBREWS 13:6

Of course, it's hard facing those situations each day—the ones that make you feel small and insignificant. Those times when you feel threatened or even humiliated. Almost like you were in *Glee* and getting a *slushie* in your face. Don't allow your confidence to be undermined. Remember that people who try to do that are really insecure themselves. Rather, rise up stronger, with more grace and dignity than your aggressors display, and keep doing what you need to be doing. God always elevates the meek and humble. But humility is not weakness. To be meek is not to be a doormat. Operate from a position of quiet strength—the courage that is defined by His presence beside you as you walk through those situations that threaten your peace.

MARCH 20

❧

Though an army besieges me, my heart will not fear; though war breaks out against me, even then I will be confident.

PSALM 27:3

Right, so you're not on top of the popularity charts. Maybe it was something you did or something you said. Maybe it's just about who you are—someone who dares to be different and stands up for the underdog. Maybe it's just that your family can't understand a choice you've made and have all come down on you like a ton of bricks. It's a difficult situation, but at this point, do not fear. Stay strong and confident. God is with you and He is for you. He loves you, strong woman, for standing up for what you believe in. He is with you every step of the way. So ride out this storm for it too shall pass. The 'army' will be defeated, and will, in due course, understand your viewpoint. Some will even switch to your side because they admire your courage. Stand strong, girl! You can do it!

MARCH 21

~

Be strong in the grace that is in Christ Jesus.

2 TIMOTHY 2:1

Remember when you thought you couldn't get a certain job done but you actually did it so well that you got a ton of compliments on how well it all turned out? Those are life's little surprises that come seemingly out of nowhere, and there are many of those that you will enjoy like welcome drops of rain when you are parched. It's called *Grace*. And it comes from Him who loves you so much that he showers you with His grace. When you're running a marathon and you wonder if you will make it through the next mile, and suddenly you get a rush of energy…that's grace. When you've made a mistake and you wonder if you can start over and He helps you over the bump in the road and tells you that you have a fresh start—that's grace…and it's there to keep you strong for the next mile. Because life is a marathon that we couldn't get through without His grace.

MARCH 22

❧

*I know whom I have believed, and
am convinced that he is able to
guard what I have entrusted to him.*

2 TIMOTHY 1:12

Well, maybe it wasn't you, but a friend, who was attracted to this new guy in school and shared some pretty deep secrets with him. Secrets she had told nobody because she didn't trust them as much as she felt she could trust this guy—because she was so bedazzled by him. Girl, if you didn't already hear the alarm bells going off when this guy sauntered into the room, then I think your hearing was probably off that day. How can anyone confide in, or trust, a person they don't know? Oh…and how it hurt when those secrets were spilled, and her trust betrayed. You cannot trust him who you do not know. Get to know your heavenly father today. Trust Him. Confide in Him. He will keep you safe from the wolves that wander amongst you in sheep's clothing. He will never betray you, but always uphold you.

MARCH 23

 ∾

Therefore, do not worry about tomorrow,
for tomorrow will worry about itself.

MATTHEW 6:34

S o, there you are, at the start of a glorious new day. The
outdoors beckons, but you are lost in thought and don't
even notice the riot of colours in the sky when you glance out
of the window. You've submitted your college applications,
or maybe you're waiting for a response to a job interview.
Waiting for the ball to bounce back and wondering how
things will play out is messing with your head. People keep
telling you to live in the moment. Well, how is that even
possible when you have to worry about tomorrow? Wait a
minute! You believe in God, don't you? So, when the Lord of
all your Tomorrows has things in the palm of His hand, why
worry? Tomorrow will take care of itself. As for you—you
have today. Make the most of this moment, girl, because it'll
be gone before you know it!

MARCH 24

Therefore, my dear brothers and sisters, stand firm. Let nothing move you. Always give yourselves fully to the work of the Lord, because you know that your labour in the Lord is not in vain.

1 CORINTHIANS 15:58

The rain falls and waters the earth. A spring bubbles up somewhere in the wilderness and slakes a weary traveller's thirst. A tree spreads out and birds take shelter in its branches, while people enjoy its shade. A plump, juicy peach falls, and someone bites into it and their energy is instantly restored. Everything that has been so carefully placed on this planet fulfils a purpose. Their existence, and what they do, is never in vain. You have been created and placed on this planet to fulfil your role as a woman. As a daughter you will lend your strength to your family. As a friend you will share your wisdom. Out in the world you will exercise sound judgement and caution…

When you step into your role with confidence, you give yourself fully to being who God meant you to be…and nothing you do ever goes in vain. More power to you, girl!

MARCH 25

*Be still before the Lord and wait
patiently for him; do not fret when
people succeed in their ways, when
they carry out their wicked schemes.*

PSALM 37:7

Why do the unjust prosper—is a question that the world has been asking for centuries. And why do the just so often seem to be oppressed. Well, it's a battle that rages on. Perhaps it's a test to see if you will stay the course and keep doing the right thing even if you don't see dividends right away. The fact is, the more you strive to do the right thing, the more you are developing a rich character, strength and resilience—all the things that define a woman. Let others do what they want to. You do what you have to—even when the meanest girl takes away the crown. The crown God has for you is far more valuable, and though you will only receive it far into the future…for now you have the assurance that He is cheering you on as you patiently go about your business.

MARCH 26

Keep your lives free from the love of money and be content with what you have, because God has said, "Never will I leave you; never will I forsake you."

HEBREWS 13:5

Lying awake at night, wondering how you will pay your bills—credit card, student loan, rent, food…you are probably fantasizing about money. It's the means to an end. It's what you need right now. It's a genuine requirement. It's not like you just want money for the sake of having it—or for the status it provides. You are working really hard, and you still have bills to pay next month. Sometimes God brings you to a place where you are forced to acknowledge that He is in control of things; and where He reminds you that He has never let you go hungry or without a roof over your head, from the day you were born. It's a place of humility, where you quietly lay your worries down and choose to relinquish control to Him. Your bills are for next month. Today's debts are paid. Tomorrow's debt will be covered too. Have faith!

MARCH 27

*Those who trust in their riches will fall, but
the righteous will thrive like a green leaf.*

PROVERBS 11:28

Ever heard of the foolish man who built his house on the
sand? Or the wise man who built his house on a rock?
No prizes for guessing whose house stood firm in the face
of a storm. Anything that is shallow has no substance and
therefore no future. To stand the test of time, you have to do
some serious digging and lay a really strong foundation. You
could call that foundation faith. Stand on it and you're like
a green leaf—full of promise, with a certain future. Because
it doesn't depend on its own strength but on the power of
its Creator. Trusting in wealth is basically leaning on your
own strength and thinking that you can do things on your
own. It's faith in false power, and that rug can be pulled out
from under your feet at any time. Less is more, in this case.
And less is often enough. Less also brings you closer to the
Provider on whom you depend. And to be close to Him is
to grow from strength to strength.

MARCH 28

❧

*Your beauty should not come from outward
adornment, such as elaborate hairstyles and
the wearing of gold jewellery or fine clothes.
Rather, it should be that of your inner self, the
unfading beauty of a gentle and quiet spirit,
which is of great worth in God's sight.*

1 PETER 3:3-4

Sigh…this is a tough pill to swallow, because us girls love our outward adornment so much. Well, you're not being asked to give it all up. You're just being directed to your inward beauty—so that when the makeup's off, you are still beautiful with that glow that shines from within. Basically, don't be overly invested in what's on the outside, but truly invest in building up and reinforcing what's on the inside. Spending time in quiet introspection and prayer will help you better understand yourself and bring to the surface all those wonderful qualities that adorn a woman of grace, strength and substance. Ultimately, it's not the outward beauty that people are attracted to, but your heart. Keep it beautiful, and you will be too!

MARCH 29

᙮

It is better to take refuge in the Lord
than to trust in humans.

PSALM 118:8

Well, you've probably had an experience or two that could testify to the unreliability of humans as opposed to the steadfastness of God. Your best friend, whom you professed to be able to trust with your life, snitched on you, made a play for the guy you are dating, or wasn't there for you when you needed her. It's not that human beings are bad. It's just that they are…well…human! God will never tell on you. He will always uplift and uphold you. He is your Father after all, and He loves you with a love that is incomparable. Girl, if you want to be truly strong, you need a strong team to back you up. That team is God. You don't need anyone else.

MARCH 30

⚜

*Therefore, I tell you, do not worry about
your life, what you will eat or drink;
or about your body, what you will
wear. Is not life more than food,
and the body more than clothes?*

MATTHEW 6:25

What thoughts occupy the most space in your mind? As you begin to answer that question, you will be shocked. What to cook, eat or shop for, have become major decisions through the day. Yet life is about so much more. Clear the shelves in your brain and replace the food with something more satisfying. Perhaps you could think about how you could be a more productive member of the community, or how you could, as the strong woman you are, bring about a change in the lives of people who are oppressed. It could just be formulating strategies to defend kids who are being bullied in your school. Food and clothes will come…and go. The impact that you make on someone's life lasts forever.

MARCH 31

*He said to her, "Daughter, your faith
has healed you. Go in peace and
be freed from your suffering."*

MARK 5:34

The father-daughter relationship is precious. How often has your dad made your cares go away with just one smile or a hug? My dear woman, there are times when you just want to sit down and have someone take care of you. That's because most often, as a woman, you just feel like you've got to keep going. Recharging your batteries is important. Taking time out and relaxing is essential. Spending time in the presence of your heavenly Father is vital… in order to stay the strong, courageous woman that you are. Remember, He's there to stop your tears, to heal your heartache, to make the pain go away. He does it quietly, gently, without judging you for mistakes you may have made. He restores you and sets you free from the shadows of the past. End this month with time spent in His presence, healing from the rigors of the past weeks…so that you can go into the next month with greater strength.

NOTES

APRIL

APRIL 1

Do not let any unwholesome talk come out of your mouths, but only what is helpful for building others up according to their needs, that it may benefit those who listen.

EPHESIANS 4:29

The power of words can never be underestimated, and sometimes you might unwittingly be tearing someone apart with what you say. Use your words to build up, and not bring down. You never know when someone's heart is breaking… and you can make their wound seem less intense with a few caring words of comfort. Words are healing. Speak positivity into someone's life today. Tell someone how much they mean to you. Or how great they look. You grow in strength as you empower others. And you're never too young to begin to take words, and their effects, seriously. Remember the times you needed to hear a word of encouragement… and how just one simple sentence was all you needed to make something you did seem all the more worthwhile!

APRIL 2

❦

How can a young person stay on the path of purity? By living according to your word.

Your life is like the sweet strains of a beautiful song that your Creator has composed for you. The lyrics of the song tell your story. As the music flows, it evokes so many emotions—laughter, tears, amusement, sorrow, regret…

Dear beautiful girl, you can make sure that your life song is unsullied by regret. The lyrics can flow like the purest mountain stream that ripples over a pristine landscape. All you need to do is to keep your ears attuned to the sound of His voice—as it guides, chides, directs and advises you.

APRIL 3

❧

Children, obey your parents in the Lord, for this is right. "Honor your father and mother"—which is the first commandment with a promise— "so that it may go well with you and that you may enjoy long life on the earth."

EPHESIANS 6:1-3

When you look up to those who have, from the moment of your birth and even before—sheltered, nurtured and nourished you, you are complete. You are stronger when you acknowledge where your strength comes from. You are reinforced when you defer to those who have given you the gift of life. One day, girl, you'll be a mother too, and things will come full circle. Give love today and it will come back to you tomorrow. Show respect and you will be respected. Obedience is simple submission to the Will of God who loves you. If you love Him, show Him how much by doing as He asks of you.

APRIL 4

❧

Listen to advice and accept
discipline, and at the end you will
be counted among the wise.

PROVERBS 19:20

You remember what happened the last time you thought you knew it all? Hmm…perhaps you don't want to be reminded about how that panned out! Strong successful women are shaped by good advice. It's really important to accept the wisdom of experience and let it soak in. It's like vitamins that give you an extra boost. Having someone tell you off isn't the most pleasant thing. Neither is having someone tell it like it is. Either way, you don't want to hear or know more. But here's the deal—if you don't listen and take note, you don't grow, and as a woman destined for great things, you need to grow or else be left behind. So, watch and learn—even when you think you know it all, because lady, there's a whole lot of knowledge and wisdom out there, and you want it to rain down on you and fill you up!

APRIL 5

～

Many are the plans in a person's heart,
but it is the Lord's purpose that prevails.

PROVERBS 19:21

Yes, you planned the date. You took matters into your own hands. You wanted to be in control. You wanted to be a strong woman of purpose and determination, and that's admirable. But things didn't go according to plan, as sometimes happens, and you wound up with a bruised ego. Don't beat yourself up over this. It's just a little blip in the larger scheme of things. You will, on many different occasions, want to put your plans before God's purpose, and He will gently guide you back. You see, He knows what's good for you and what is detrimental. Chances are that after the really bad date that you had planned and taken control of, you discovered that wasn't the person for you after all. Well, God knew that. His purpose often doesn't fall in line with your plans. So maybe it's time to align your plans with His purpose.

APRIL 6

⁓

For our light and momentary troubles
are achieving for us an eternal glory
that far outweighs them all.

2 CORINTHIANS 4:17

Remember that meal you cooked that people said was the best they'd ever had? I wonder what they would have thought if they had peeked behind the scenes…and seen the pans you flung across the room in frustration when the recipe just wasn't working…the flour in your hair and up to your elbows; your grease stained, tear stained apron; the finger you almost sliced off when you were trying to chop onions like a chef. And suddenly—things just came together, and by the time your friends arrived, the meal looked like something out of a cook book—picture perfect and so delicious. That's what life's like. You have to go through the mess in order to attain that moment of glory.

APRIL 7

～

So we fix our eyes not on what is seen, but on what is unseen, since what is seen is temporary, but what is unseen is eternal.

2 CORINTHIANS 4:18

This may sound strange to you, but some of the things that people leave unsaid, or some of the feelings that go undemonstrated, sometimes mean more than all the words and actions in the world. Value the gentle look of understanding; the words between the lines. They come from a good place. And that good place is an eternal place that reflects the very love and heart of God. We find ourselves so busy chasing the obvious amidst the noise of the world, when the truth that fills the silence is left unexplored. Today, think about how much time you spend on things and emotions that are here today, gone tomorrow, and how much time you are investing in relationships and people who will impact your life in the long run.

APRIL 8

Because of the Lord's great love we are not consumed, for his compassions never fail. They are new every morning.

LAMENTATIONS 3:22-23

When you're dragging your feet home after yet another argument or misunderstanding with a friend or a loved one, think about how light it will make you feel to forgive, forget and move on. And please, don't give me the *"I might forgive but I won't forget"* spiel. Because that won't cut it. Rather, every time you feel aggrieved and hurt, remember God's compassion that wipes your slate clean and gives you a fresh start every day. Give someone else a fresh start. Wipe the slate clean. You'll feel lighter and stronger.

APRIL 9

❧

My flesh and my heart may fail,
but God is the strength of my
heart and my portion forever.

PSALM 73:26

When the going gets tough…you get going girl! Don't let anything or anyone keep you down! The road to your future is fraught with challenges but you know what? They're the best thing that will happen to you because they will shape who you will become. They will make you the vibrant, interesting, amazing person you were meant to be. When you're on a roll, enjoy the ride. When you hit a wall, wait patiently for it to crumble before your perseverance. When you're down, you get up and put your best foot forward—and that's even when it hurts. You might not be superwoman, but you're a *super woman* and you get your strength from God—who lives within you, and who wants to take your hand and help you across the next mile and over the next hurdle.

APRIL 10

❧

The Lord is my strength and my shield;
my heart trusts in him, and he helps me.
My heart leaps for joy, and with
my song I praise him.

PSALM 28:7

I magine that you're camping outdoors, sitting before a gently crackling fire; toasting marshmallows perhaps, while you swap stories with your friends. There are stars above, and the green earth below you. Somewhere around and about you know there may be a wild animal or two… but being out there in this beautiful slice of heaven makes you feel quite unafraid and unthreatened by anything. Go back to this place in your mind whenever you feel afraid. Remember that God is all around you—in the air you breathe and even the situation you are in. Just say thank you to Him. You'll be amazed at how your heart will leap when you express your gratitude. You'll feel stronger, in control, and able to get past just about anything!

APRIL 11

❧

*Look to the Lord and his strength;
seek his face always.*

1 CHRONICLES 16:11

There's something immensely soothing about watching the waves rippling towards the shore. There's a strength within them that you know exists. You feel that power beneath you when you're surfing, and you feel it even if you're just wading in the shallows. They reflect the strength and power of the Creator. Just like the wind does. It can be a gentle breeze, or it can be a driving wind. And whether it's the wind or the waves, you can see God in them. Just as you can in all of nature. So, go out every once in a while… and feel the sun on your face and the breeze in your hair. Be close to the Author of Life and draw on His strength.

APRIL 12

❧

It is God who arms me with strength,
And makes my way perfect.

PSALM 18:32

Moving away from something or someone—home, loved ones or even old ways and habits, takes strength. Every day there is a battle—especially when you are striving to put away old habits and are fighting to stay on top of the situation. At such a time it helps to remember that God endows or arms you with the strength and resolve that you need. You might not be able to make it on your own, but with Him you can do the impossible. He clears the path ahead of you and gently leads you over the obstacles. When you feel weary He uplifts you and refreshes your soul. Today, place your hand in His. Don't stumble in the dark anymore. Be strengthened, nourished and reinforced in Him.

APRIL 13

I have told you these things, so that in me you may have peace. In this world you will have trouble. But take heart! I have overcome the world.

JOHN 16:33

The thing about life is that it's filled with noise. The noise of events taking place all around you. The noise of hectic activity. The noise of your own thoughts. Added to this noise is the babble of hundreds of voices—some of which continually address you in your head—come here, go there, do this, don't do that. You can strive to escape from the commotion, but no matter which direction you run, you can never get away. But when you rest in Him…when you lie down and drift into the peace of His presence, the sounds of the world recede; leaving in their wake a peace that cannot be defined. It's the peace that comes from walking, talking and being with The One who has overcome the world. May you lean into that peace today and let go of all your cares.

APRIL 14

❧

God is our refuge and strength,
an ever-present help in trouble.
Therefore we will not fear...

PSALM 46:1-3

If you've ever lived close to your grandparents, you'll know the unparalleled joy of running to them to escape the discipline of a parent. Hiding behind grandma is like being in a safe haven where nothing can touch you. You are protected. You have no need to fear. In the larger scheme of things, God provides that refuge. He beckons to you to hide in the shelter of His presence so that you are spared the buffeting of this world's troubles. Today, as you wonder how you will face those problems looming up ahead of you, remember that He protects you. You have no need to fear.

APRIL 15

*We continually ask God to fill you
with the knowledge of his will through
all the wisdom and understanding
that the Spirit gives...*

COLOSSIANS 1:9

Confidence in yourself comes from doing the right thing...and from pursuing that which is best for you. Pursuing what will ultimately result in your good, is exercising wisdom and understanding, which every woman needs and yearns for. So what do you do when the Will of your Creator clashes with your own desires? Well, you're at crossroads and confused about which way to go. Ultimately you are given a choice. What will your choice be? Will you choose His Will and operate in wisdom, or go your own way and miss out? Girl, be cautious. Choose Him every time for a truly rich and fulfilling life.

APRIL 16

~⌇

I pray that out of his glorious riches he may strengthen you with power through his Spirit in your inner being.

EPHESIANS 3:16

Being broke is the worst thing. It's almost paralysing. Imagine if you never had to go through that. Now think about being spiritually broke. With nothing in your spiritual bank to draw from. That would be not only paralysing, but devastating. Not having spiritual wealth to draw from leaves you unfulfilled and in a constant state of drought. Living right, working diligently and trusting in God to supply all your needs, gives you financial stability. Stay close to the source of all light and your surroundings are illuminated. Stay close to the Giver of all good things and you will be filled. Start today with a prayer—that you will always steward your resources well, listening to the voice of reason when it comes to spending…and always remembering that to be spiritually rich is to be wealthy indeed.

APRIL 17

⁓

But remember the Lord your God, for it is He who gives you the ability to produce wealth, and so confirms his covenant, which he swore to your ancestors, as it is today.

DEUTERONOMY 8:18

When the cobwebs clear from your brain, and sleep is washed from your eyes, bring yourself to ponder this truth—that the results of all that work, striving and aspiring, that you gave yourself credit for, wasn't you at all. It was Him —in you. If you want to increase your productivity, dedicate your work to Him. Dedicate all of your life to Him. He keeps His promises and He will not go back on His word. Your success is defined by your ability to rely on God's provision, and by your acknowledgment of the role He plays in planning your life and realizing your aspirations. Your heavenly father wants only good things for you and He ensures that you have them.

APRIL 18

❧

But the Lord stood at my
side and gave me strength.

2 TIMOTHY 4:17

Often, when you're flagging and about to give up, there is a fresh spurt of energy just about to be discharged. A boost that will catapult you to greater success. This is God's prize for not falling by the wayside, and for dusting yourself off and staying the course. Disappointment is something you will encounter at various seasons in your life. How you handle it is key to what you will take from it. It's important not to allow it to defeat you, but rather to use it as motivation to keep going. Keep that finish line in view and believe that ahead of you is a victory like no other. Like springs that well up and feed a river, let your faith rise up within you and flow into your veins with the strength and power to start over and do even better than you did before. Each time you get to the end of your strength, God gives you some of His. That's why the rush of energy you feel when you're just about to fall, but didn't, is unlike anything you will ever experience. So you keep going, lady. There's glory ahead of you!

APRIL 19

Take delight in the Lord, and he will give you the desires of your heart.

PSALM 37:4

Well, we know you've got your list for Santa all ready—though it's months yet till Christmas! The fact is, we all have those long lists and just wish we could have somebody come down the chimney and give us all the things we have been dreaming of. Keep those lists. But build the chimney—that conduit of faith that lies just above the fire of your rejoicing in all things impossible. A lot of things seem impossible in your hands, but in the hands of God, they take on a whole new dimension. Trust Him. He is the best provider ever!

APRIL 20

Fight the good fight of the faith.
Take hold of the eternal life to
which you were called...

1 TIMOTHY 6:12

Think about a well. They don't have them around anymore—certainly not the kind you see in picture books, with the bucket suspended above it. Have an imaginary well in your head at all times. Believe me, it's a great place to go to. You can lower the bucket and be revived and refreshed. You can sit on the edge and have a conversation about life. You can gaze into the depths and marvel at how, no matter the quantity of water you draw out, there's still more to draw, and more... it never runs out. That's a picture of eternal life. You can sample it today and savour it forever. All that is required is that you keep coming to the well and drawing from it.

APRIL 21

❦

*Whatever you do, work at it with all
your heart, as working for the Lord, not
for human masters, since you know that
you will receive an inheritance from
the Lord as a reward. It is the
Lord Christ you are serving.*

COLOSSIANS 3:23-24

Have you heard your grandma saying, '*work is worship*?
Well, that's true. So all the hard work you put in at
school or work, is being assessed and appreciated by God.
That's pretty cool to think about, isn't it? On the other hand, if
you're skipping classes or not going regularly to work, well…
you know who you're going to have to answer to! How do
you think about work? How do you approach an assignment?
It's a good point for introspection today. Whatever you do,
do it cheerfully and wholeheartedly, and you will see the
results match the effort.

APRIL 22

~

Do not conform to the pattern of this world, but be transformed by the renewing of your mind. Then you will be able to test and approve what God's will is— his good, pleasing and perfect will.

ROMANS 12:2

If you can't recognise yourself when you take a look in the mirror, if what you imbibed the other night still makes you feel ill when you think of it; if you have a bunch of friends with whom you have absolutely nothing in common, but you're hanging with them simply because it's the cool thing to do…that's peer pressure. It's the *'fit in or keep out'* syndrome. It's the bogeyman that lurks in the hallways of every school, and maybe even by the coffee machine at work. It's as scary as the bogeyman and just as destructive to your peace of mind. Yet, Christ calls you to move away from the pack and to be different. To be transformed, in order to do His Will. Today, think about taking that first step towards doing something that builds you up. You will see yourself, and life itself, in a more positive light.

APRIL 23

Long life is in her right hand;
in her left hand are riches and honor.

PROVERBS 3:16

Ah sweet girl, just take a look at yourself and love what you see. The beauty that you've been blessed with. The intellect, the grace, the exceptional ability to love and nurture. Have you thanked God for all of that today? Or have you spent an inordinately long time wishing you could change everything from the top of your head to the soles of your feet…when He created you and pronounced you perfect? Maybe you're not the model in the pages of a magazine… or the high achiever on the television screen. But they're not you either. And maybe if they saw you, they would wish to be you. But that's not how it was meant to be. Each beautiful woman has her place. You have yours and they have theirs. So today, celebrate who you are and where you're going, because girl, you're going places!

APRIL 24

~

Her ways are pleasant ways,
and all her paths are peace.

PROVERBS 3:17

Sisterhood is a gift. Girls hanging out together—wow, that's a thing of joy indeed. It's worth remembering, and reminding yourself, at this point, that these moments together are like gold. Value them. They are so precious. Let nothing diminish the joy you find in each other's company. Women actually gain strength from each other. Your sisters are the ones you can talk to about anything. They understand where you're coming from and they give you good advice. Always remember that each woman is unique. When you realise how perfect you are in your own unique way that God determined, you are better able to accept others and celebrate them.

APRIL 25

～c

She is a tree of life to those who take hold of her; those who hold her fast will be blessed.

S trong woman—you are like a tree whose roots are firmly embedded in the earth! Maybe you don't always feel that way, but it's the truth! The secret to your success is to always find your way back to who you are meant to be. Someone who is grounded. Someone who others turn to for strength, because you have so much to give. Yeah, no pressure there! However, like the tree, your roots need nourishment—they need to draw on the richness of the soil they are embedded in. What is the strength that you are drawing on? What is the nature of the soil that your roots are reaching into? Draw on the richness of God's word. Stay rooted in His promises. Though the storms may toss you, your roots will stay firm, and your branches (or all who cling to you for strength) will not waver.

APRIL 26

Everything is possible for one who believes.

MARK 9:23

When you need strength, you build your muscles. When you need more Faith, you exercise your belief. Belief is inspired by trust in the promises of God. Belief is rooted in the word of God. Belief challenges the norm and expects the impossible to happen even in the direst conditions. When you see a flower bloom in the desert, that reinforces belief in all things impossible. When you see someone change and transform, that strengthens your trust in the impossible. Belief is the hope that tomorrow will be better than today. It is trusting that you will be more able to accomplish everything that you want to. Do you have faith? Do you believe? Do you trust? Think about these three words today. They make everything possible.

APRIL 27

❧

*Therefore, I urge you, brothers and sisters,
in view of God's mercy, to offer your bodies
as a living sacrifice, holy and pleasing to
God—this is your true and proper worship.*

ROMANS 12:1

Lovely lady, I know the pressures that you are under. Scrolling through Instagram and Facebook gives you an unrealistic view of what you need to expect of yourself. You've been hitting the gym every morning and dieting, and your efforts have not gone unnoticed. God loves you to be disciplined and to take care of yourself. But think about why you are working so hard. Is it to meet some ideal that you have of what a woman should look like? Or is it to keep yourself fit and healthy? Keep your expectations of yourself realistic, then you will also be more accepting of others... as well as of yourself. You are not defined by an Instagram post, but by how you are treating yourself. Are you respecting yourself and your body? Think about this today and let God show you how He sees you—wonderfully made!

APRIL 28

❧

Whoever dwells in the shelter of the Most High will rest in the shadow of the Almighty. I will say of the Lord, "He is my refuge and my fortress, my God, in whom I trust."

When you were a little girl, you may have had an experience of being afraid of something or someone… and your daddy said he would come with you and stand by your side, or right behind you, as you tackled that fear. Your heavenly daddy gives you a similar reassurance—that He is always there by your side, shielding you. With Him in your corner, you can rest—really rest and not worry about a thing. He eases the stress away. If you have a problem, you can talk to Him about it and He will help you. Only have faith. Trust that He listens and is acting upon your requests even as you are speaking. It's the most natural place in all the world to be—safe in the shadow of God. A house that stands in the shadow of a mountain is safe. The mountain defends and protects it from the wind, the rain and the storm.

APRIL 29

~c

He will cover you with his feathers,
and under his wings you will
find refuge; his faithfulness will
be your shield and rampart.

PSALM 91:4

Being brave when you're feeling anything but courageous is the hardest thing. Especially when people around you expect you to suck it up and keep that smile on your face. While your facial muscles are stretched to their limit, so are your nerves and everything else inside of you. Your system is, quite simply put, in an unnatural state. It's okay to be vulnerable, and it's okay to be out of it while you deal with things that may have thrown you off balance. Truly strong people acknowledge and face moments of weakness. The strength is in getting yourself together once you have been through the process of dealing with your emotions…and moving on, stronger than ever before, in Him.

APRIL 30

~

The Lord will keep you from all harm—
he will watch over your life; the Lord will
watch over your coming and going
both now and forevermore.

PSALM 121:7-8

Travelling on your own, whether on a journey or in life, might sometimes fill you with anxiety. You're wondering if you'll be safe; if the terrain you are travelling through will be hospitable or hostile, and if you will find friendly faces to go on the journey with you. God has a plan. He mapped your path. He set you on it, and He steers the course. He watches over you; anticipating each challenge along the route, and prepares you for it. If you are facing a problem of some kind at the moment, this is His way of getting you fit for the next leg of the journey. He is with you as you undergo each endurance test and each test of your loyalty and commitment. Don't waste precious energy on worry. He is with you, and He will get you where you need to be.

NOTES

_____

_____

_____

_____

_____

_____

_____

_____

_____

_____

_____

_____

_____

MAY

MAY 1

❧

*Do to others as you would
have them do to you.*

LUKE 6:31

You feel like you're going to burst. You can't wait to tell that person off. It doesn't feel good to be this angry. It's making your breath come faster and your blood vessels seem constricted. If you were any angrier, your heart would be in big trouble. Oh, but you want to erupt because you are so incensed at being treated so unfairly. Stop, exhale, take a drink of water and splash some of that cool liquid on your face. Let your facial muscles relax. Try to smile. Alright, if you need to punch a cushion, you may. Now sit down, lean back and breathe. It's okay. The moment has passed… and God is smiling down on you. You didn't give in to your anger. You wouldn't have liked it if someone else had erupted on you the way you were planning to blow up on someone. So, you've done the right thing. You've decided to exhale and release the anger. Girl, you've just done yourself a huge favour.

MAY 2

Do not be misled: Bad company
corrupts good character

1 CORINTHIANS 15:33

You've got this really close friend but maybe she's just not doing things right. Maybe her lifestyle bothers you. Perhaps she means well, but she has some bad habits, and instead of indulging in them herself, she tries to draw you in. Because you care about her so much, you try your best to get her to change. You give her all the good advice that you can, and you really spend time trying to explain how her life choices are harming her. You try and she doesn't listen. You persist, but then she gets defensive. Maybe it's time to let go and save yourself from further heartache and protect yourself from that self-destructive path that your friend is on. Keep praying that she will allow God to save her.

MAY 3

❧

One who has unreliable friends
soon comes to ruin, but there is
a friend who sticks closer

PROVERBS 18:24

You know that friend who tells it like it is? The one who shakes her head and tells you quite frankly that you are making a huge mistake, or that your dress is dreadful, or you're wearing too much make-up? Well, that's the friend you need to keep close. She is like gold—closer than a sister. Keep the ingenuine friends far away. The ones who gush all the time and tell you how wonderful you are. They're probably saying the opposite the moment your back is turned. The honest friend will be there for you when the chips are down. She will tell you frankly how you have made a fool of yourself, but she will also tell you how you can turn things around. The other friends will avoid you. Some will even pretend not to know you. You might not think so, but they're doing you a favour. Having one friend who holds up a mirror for you to look into, is far more valuable than all the fake friends in the world.

MAY 4

❧

He will wipe every tear from their eyes

REVELATION 21:4

One day the pain will cease. One day all sorrows will come to an end. Right now, life is often hard and there are a lot of emotions you have to deal with every day—most especially when you're hormonal and feeling particularly vulnerable. Try to process your emotions productively. Which doesn't mean that you use your family and friends as punching bags, but rather that you distance yourself from the situation and assess it dispassionately. Sorry to have to tell you this but hurt through betrayal and insincerity are a normal part of life. It's particularly traumatic when they come at you from out of the blue. If you need to cry, get the tears out without allowing yourself to be submerged or overwhelmed by your emotions. Yes, one day there'll be no more pain and tears. For now…take them to God.

MAY 5

❧

Walk with the wise and become wise,
for a companion of fools suffers harm

PROVERBS 13:20

Sure, it would be great if we all had the wise King Solomon to hang out with. We would stay close until we soaked up all his wisdom. Not that we're making light of this truth—that the people you choose to hang out with will ultimately influence your life. It's just important to understand that we all have to put in some effort into choosing good friends and mentors. They might not have the wisdom of Solomon, but if they are grounded and level-headed; have good values and a close relationship with God, they will have a good influence on you. And woman, you have innate wisdom. Don't you ever forget that. Share it as often as you can. Be a positive influence in someone's life today!

MAY 6

Better is open rebuke than hidden love.
Wounds from a friend can be trusted,
but an enemy multiplies kisses

PROVERBS 27:5-6

Value the frank opinions of good friends. Treasure the people who do not mince their words but speak out because they love you and think you need censure and correction for your own good. You might feel hurt for a while and go away to lick your wounds in private, but when you have thought things through, you will realise the benefit of sincerity. Honest reproof is better than honey coated words that are empty of value. And if the shoe is on the other foot and there is someone you love who is doing something foolish and needs her eyes opened, don't be afraid. Even if she turns her back on you for a while, your words would have hit home and she will thank you for them one day. Honesty pays every time.

MAY 7

❦

A friend loves at all times, and a brother
(or sister!) is born for a time of adversity

PROVERBS 17:17

There is a solemn truth that you will learn soon, if you haven't already done so. It is that you will know who your friends are when all is not so rosy in your world. As long as you're on top, people flock around you. You're popular. But when you're going through tough times, it is only the real friends who stick around to help you through rough weather. Fake friends fail you and bail on you. Genuine friends will stick with you—even in a sinking boat—and fight the storm with you. Throw a party and you'll have a crowd. Be in mourning and you will find out who really cares for you. Now put the shoe on the other foot and ask yourself—am I being a sister to someone who is facing a time of adversity? Have I visited my friend who lost a loved one? Have I called the friend who had to drop out of school? Have I been a source of comfort and help to someone today?

MAY 8

❧

*As iron sharpens iron, so one
person sharpens another.*

PROVERBS 27:17

Life is short, so be prudent about how you spend your time. Be especially discerning about who you spend your time with, because the kind of friends you have will ultimately determine the kind of person you will be. Choose to hang out with people who are honest. Those who don't pull any punches, and want the best for you, even if it means telling you something you don't want to hear. Those are the ones who will stick by you when times get rough. Today, think about all the people in your life and call someone who was honest with you because, above everything else, they genuinely cared for your wellbeing.

MAY 9

~

The righteous choose their friends carefully.

PROVERBS 12:26

Destructive relationships are devastating. They also disempower you. True friends, on the other hand, build you up and reinforce your belief in yourself. Maybe you're smarting from something that someone said or did to you that was a blow to your self esteem. It's important to differentiate between those who intentionally hurt you and those who express their opinions honestly because they want the best for you. You want to be open to constructive advice, but steer clear of the people who seek to hammer away at your confidence.

MAY 10

~

Let my teaching fall like rain and my words descend like dew, like showers on new grass, like abundant rain on tender plants.

DEUTERONOMY 32:2

Dear daughter of God, may you know wisdom today. Don't look for it in the pages of a magazine, and especially not on social media. Find it in the eyes of a grandparent or in the voice of a parent, sibling or friend who cares about you. Discover it in The Word of Him who is above all things—who breathed life into you and formed you in His image. Wisdom lies beneath the layers of experience, and echoes in the voices of those who have lived and learned. It doesn't blow in the wind but resides in those hidden places that you have yet to discover. When Wisdom comes knocking, open the door quickly. Don't miss the sound of the knocking—don't let it be lost in the babble of voices in your head.

MAY 11

✦

I will proclaim the name of the Lord.
Oh, praise the greatness of our God!

DEUTERONOMY 32:3

Being grateful, when there seems little to celebrate, is hard. We all know how hollow our voices sound when the storm clouds loom overhead and the world seems dark—with dreams falling apart, plans in disarray, and everybody else appearing to have it all together except you. But girl, there's truth in the statement that when you declare gratitude in the face of adversity, it drives the clouds away. The rain stops and the sun comes out. Simply by refusing to acknowledge the negativity of the situation, you've reversed it! Praising your Creator—being thankful for the fact that you are living and breathing—and acknowleding His greatness, can actually change the atmosphere and transform the outcome of things. So go ahead—shout out a hallelujah!

MAY 12

❧

He is the Rock, his works are perfect,
and all his ways are just.

DEUTERONOMY 32:4

At times it may seem like there's nobody in the world that you can rely on. Perhaps it's because you have been let down multiple times, and have lost trust even in those closest to you. You feel submerged by a rather large wave of cynicism. At that point the world, and everyone in it, seems to disappoint you. This is not your day, your week, your month, even your year, perhaps. So you're waiting for something, or someone, to change your outlook… little realising that the only one who can do that is you. Shift focus. Turn your gaze upwards. Discover the rock on which you can stand strong, without the rug being pulled out from under your feet. Enjoy the perfection of each day—you will find it if you seek it, because He created all things to be perfect. And reassure yourself that life is fair—because He who is 'just' created it. All you need to do is simply look at things differently.

MAY 13

❧

Ask your father and he will tell you,
your elders, and they will explain to you.

DEUTERONOMY 32:7

What truth are you seeking today? Is it to do with the purpose of your life or advice on a course of action that you need to take? It's alright not to know all the answers. It's okay to feel overwhelmed at times. The answers will come—perhaps not immediately, but always at the right time. All you need to to is to trust that Higher Power to give you insights and to unveil knowledge as you go along. I know you probably wish for the path to be clear, but it often isn't. It unfolds one step at a time, so just keep going and you will find your way to the answers.

MAY 14

❧

When you go to war against your enemies and see horses and chariots and an army greater than yours, do not be afraid of them, because the Lord your God, who brought you up out of Egypt, will be with you.

DEUTERONOMY 20:1

Yes, your opponent's arsenal generally appears more substantial than your own. Maybe that girl you wish you were, has been getting better grades and seems more accomplished. Maybe someone else got the promotion you were hoping for. What you need to do, when you find yourself feeling dwarfed by someone else's achievements, is to look at how far you have come. Your path was fraught with challenges, but you made it through. Even the way forward seems to be tough to traverse, but you can do it. Never allow yourself to be intimidated by circumstances, because you have the God of heaven's armies on your side and your Heavenly Father will make a way for you.

MAY 15

The Lord bless you, my daughter.

RUTH 3:10

I hope you are feeling on top of the world today. Maybe you don't feel like you're particularly blessed, but you are. The more you think about it, the more you will realise it. Girl, you've got something nobody else does—you, your uniqueness and your potential. Begin to realise this and you will be like that butterfly emerging from its cocoon. Today, spread your wings and fly—do something different. Do something that celebrates who you are. And spread a little sunshine on somebody else as well. What goes around comes around. The positivity that emanates from you will return to you a hundredfold in the form of friends, popularity and joy.

MAY 16

❧

And now, my daughter, don't be afraid.
I will do for you all you ask. All the
people of my town know that you
are a woman of noble character.

RUTH 3:11

There's a promise that you have been born with. A declaration made as your first cry was heard. It is the constant reassurance that your heavenly father will answer your every request. Your strength is defined by how much, and how frequently, you remember this promise. He gives you the ability to deal with just about anything—whether it's the taunts of those who think themselves to be better or more talented; or whether it is the betrayal or disappointment you may experience from time to time. Remember this too— you were born to be a woman of noble character. Make no mistake, this is a fact. Now go out there and live it.

MAY 17

❧

So God created mankind in his own image,
in the image of God he created them.

GENESIS 1:27

Concerned about your image? Wondering how to look like those girls whose images are splashed all over social media? Those photographs that make you feel insecure, inadequate and inept, all at the same time? Take a break from self-criticism today and focus on your strengths. There's one super strength that you seem to have forgotten—God created you in His image. You are His daughter, and a child inevitably resembles her parent. Today, take one strength—be it a physical attribute, talent or accomplishment, and celebrate it. Rather than lamenting all that you don't have, shout joyfully about all that you possess…because you have what somebody else admires and aspires to have. Ultimately, we're all looking at each other… and it's like we're looking in the mirror—because we are all created in His image.

MAY 18

*God saw all that he had
made, and it was very good.*

The thing about yourself that you need to remember, and repeat often to yourself, is that God is well pleased with His handiwork. He formed and fashioned you in His own image, and He pronounced that you were not just good, but very good. Even when you're having a bad hair day or have inexplicably gained a pound or two, you are very good. Because God sees you as you probably need to see yourself—through the eyes of love. Today, say *'I love you'* to yourself. And really mean it. Tell yourself all that you love about you—from your eyes to your smile, to that crinkle in your nose when you laugh. And when you truly begin to love yourself, you will find people attracted to you. To be popular with others, be popular with yourself first.

MAY 19

⁓

The Lord God said, "It is not good for the man to be alone. I will make a helper suitable for him."

GENESIS 2:18

Okay, so you decided not to test your culinary skills and ordered takeout instead. You were planning to listen to your date talk about himself, but instead he asked you about yourself and you didn't stop talking until you saw that glazed look in his eye. In your mind the date was a disaster, and you wonder if you will ever see this guy again. You have this preconceived idea about the ideal woman, but what you need to realise is that there's no one size fits all. God *custom made* you for someone. If it's this guy you went on a date with, then be sure that he will be calling you…because he likes you just the way you are and wouldn't change a thing about you.

MAY 20

❧

*Do not seek revenge or bear a
grudge against anyone among your
people, but love your neighbour as yourself.*

LEVITICUS 19:18

Holding a grudge and seeking revenge can literally give you wrinkles ahead of time. Harbouring anything toxic within yourself affects everything about you. It especially casts a shadow on your appearance. Fill your heart with forgiveness, and your face will radiate the light of love. To be popular and loved by your peers, you need to love them first. Hostility breeds hostility. Love inspires love. People will hurt you—both intentionally and unintentionally. Let it go. Neither hold it, nor toss it back. Don't give hurt and hurtful behaviour any place in your life. It's like poison, and you don't want to imbibe it. Instead, side-step, when the venom is hurled at you, and let it fall on the floor. Then crush it beneath your six-inch heels and sashay away to freedom!

MAY 21

~

For the Lord gives wisdom, from his mouth come knowledge and understanding.

PROVERBS 2:6

Hey, remember a few days ago when we talked about you being made in God's image? A pretty cool thought, huh? Well, even more incredible, is that He gives you wisdom, knowledge and understanding. Did you hear that, lady? Did somebody make you feel inadequate or stupid lately? Shrug that feeling off and instead wear this truth like an armour. That you were created in your heavenly daddy's image and He never designed you to be inadequate. All those negative views of yourself come from the world. They feed you the lies, and you're only being stupid when you believe them. Be wise and declare the truth. That you have ability and intelligence—that comes from Him who desires only the best for you.

MAY 22

❧

Blessed are those who find wisdom,
those who gain understanding.

PROVERBS 3:13

Someone said something to you that made you really angry—and you rose to the bait. You retaliated in kind, and showed them a side of you that you don't ever want anybody to see. Oh dear, you'd been working so hard to transform that part of you and it just came out at the most inopportune moment. Girl, that's because you just suppressed a side of you that you knew wasn't pretty. The lesson to be learned is this—anything that you have inside of you will invariably come out, one way or the other. You can't keep it in forever. Instead, seek wisdom and understanding to permanently eliminate that anger or resentment, so that the next time you are taunted, you shrug your elegant shoulders and walk away.

MAY 23

❧

By wisdom a house is built, and through understanding it is established...

PROVERBS 24:3-4

When you're building anything—a relationship, a career, or even your finances, you need both wisdom and understanding. *Wisdom* to exercise your intuition and *understanding* of the resources you are working with. You can save yourself a lot of trouble and heartache if you assiduously pursue these two attributes and make them the pillars you cling onto. They hold you up, and they even keep you afloat when the seas are rough. There will always be challenges in life, but with wisdom and understanding you can surmount obstacles with grace and dignity. Woman, you're a conqueror. The only weapons you need are these two—wisdom and understanding!

MAY 24

Whoever walks in integrity walks securely.

PROVERBS 10:9

The world is a jungle at times—and you are the prey. It's easy to assume an approach that befits the environment you are in. Some call it 'dog eat dog'…while others call it survival of the fittest. Amidst all of this, remember who you are in Him who gave you life. Woman, there's no glory in stomping on someone else to climb up to where you want to be. Give someone a hand instead and be where you were meant to be! What you attain will be far more permanent. Far more valuable. Integrity is a truly valuable characteristic that defines who you are as a woman. Hold it close to you—it will keep you from falling!

MAY 25

*The way of the Lord is a
refuge for the blameless.*

PROVERBS 10:29

So, somebody said you were to blame for the mess. It could be a quarrel or misunderstanding, and now you feel like everywhere you go, or whatever you say, you just seem to get it all wrong, and end up being the one everybody is pointing their fingers at. It's ok. Dust yourself off and keep going. Smile. Shrug off the blame. You meant well and they didn't understand. Take refuge in the promises of God. He always thinks the best of you and desires that you be happy. Walk in the path He designed for you. Even if you stumble, He will pick you up. Today, be good to yourself. And smile at the people who point their fingers at you. You do what's right. It will make you feel on top of the world.

MAY 26

❧

I will give you a wise and discerning heart.

1 KINGS 3:12

Maybe you're wondering why you have a heart at all—it's liable to be hurt, broken and mistreated. Perhaps you wish you could protect it. Especially after somebody has stomped all over it and thrown it back at you. So what does a wise and discerning heart really mean? Is it insured against pain? No, it's the same heart, but it knows how to protect itself when it needs to. It invites the covering of God's love, that enables it to love wisely and with discernment. It elevates you rather than brings you down. It goes out to those deserving of your love and those who desperately need your care and concern. It is kind and compassionate, and uplifts the downcast. Today, acknowledge the goodness of your heart. Celebrate the heart of a wise woman.

MAY 27

Lord, listen! Lord, forgive! Lord,
hear and act!

DANIEL 9:19

Rough week? Wondering what's going to come at you next? Well, for a start, don't plan on stepping out with your hair in a mess and your makeup smeared. When you're feeling like this, it's the day you dress with extra care. And as you get ready and are looking in the mirror, talk to yourself, and cry out to God. Give yourself a pep talk. Remind yourself how strong you are and how you are even stronger with the strength that God pours into you when you're flagging. If you've done something you aren't proud of, talk to God about it. Tell Him what you're going through. He is loving and forgiving. He hears you when you cry out to Him, and He will make a way.

MAY 28

❧

May your God, whom you serve continually, rescue you!

DANIEL 6:16

Have you taken on too much? Are you struggling to get things done? Are you forgetting to enjoy life in the midst of all the stress? You mean well...and you really are doing the best you can, but you feel like you're sinking. Don't panic. Just take a moment to step back and take stock—regroup and begin to prioritise. It's difficult doing what you're doing, and you definitely need help. Trust that God will rescue you. You will get the task done. You will accomplish what you set out to. You will reach those all important milestones.

MAY 29

*Those who are wise will shine like
the brightness of the heavens.*

DANIEL 12:3

How often have you felt that you could do with just a little more wisdom? Maybe in your youthful effervescence you jumped into something you shouldn't have. It could be committing to something or someone that you couldn't fulfill your obligation to, and that hurt. It was difficult to acknowledge that you may have been reckless or hasty and possibly didn't think things through the way you should have. Be kind to yourself. You're not perfect. Nobody is. You made a mistake and you learned from it. That's how wisdom is born.

MAY 30

❧

*I thank and praise you, God of
my ancestors… You have given
me wisdom and power.*

DANIEL 2:23

While meditating on wisdom, and how much you need it every day, it's surprising to think that many a time you actually fail to acknowledge that you have it. You may be young, but you have inherent wisdom given to you by God who bestowed it upon you like a mantle of protection. You recognise that you possess it when you make a good decision or realise when you've made a bad one. You know you have it when you choose one set of friends over another or make lifestyle choices that may even surprise you. Wisdom is power—just like knowledge. Use it well today.

MAY 31

Fear not, peace be with you; be strong and of good courage.

DANIEL 10:19

You have come to the end of another month—stronger, more confident, and aware that you are endowed with wisdom and understanding. Tomorrow the door opens to another month. Approach it with confidence and hope. Toss apprehensions out of the window and tell yourself that no matter what's up ahead you will handle it like the strong, confident, courageous woman that you are. Keep walking tall—and I don't just mean on your high heels! Square your shoulders and look the world in the eye. With God on your side you are more than a conqueror!

NOTES

JUNE

JUNE 1

Let all that you do be done in love.

1 CORINTHIANS 16:14

If you see someone who needs a smile, give them one of yours. If someone is angry, see the hurt that they are hiding. If someone is silent, look beneath the surface to see all the pain that they are holding in—so much so that they feel too choked to say a word. Remember, this life is not just about you. It's about what you were put on this planet to do. You may not always feel like an ambassador of peace or a giver of joy, but to someone out there, you are all of those things. It's vital to remember that you are probably the bright spot in someone's day, and the person they look to for a kind word or a piece of advice. Freely you have received God's love. Freely bestow it on others.

JUNE 2

❧

Let the morning bring me word of your
unfailing love, for I have put my trust in you.

PSALM 143:8

At the end of a dark night of tossing and turning, questioning your self-worth and wondering if there is anybody at all in the world you cares for you…greet the dawn with thanksgiving for the unfailing love of a faithful God. Today, think about what you are placing your trust in. Is it in people who will let you down or things that will inevitably lose their allure? You know how little value that gives your life. Instead, place your trust in your Father God who will give you the kind of joy and fulfillment that will last for ever. It's like standing on solid ground as opposed to treading on quicksand.

JUNE 3

❧

Show me the way I should go,
for to you I entrust my life.

PSALM 143:8

When you're seeking inspiration or guidance, it's normal to look to someone you know rather than sending a prayer heavenwards. But your Creator is the only one who can actually advise you—because He knows you intimately and has already mapped out your life. Rather than taking a false step and having to start all over again, go to the Author of the route map and ask for directions. He is, after all, the only one you can trust with your life.

JUNE 4

◦⌒◦

Let love and faithfulness never leave you;
bind them around your neck, write
them on the tablet of your heart.

P R O V E R B S   3 : 3 - 4

Faithfulness is the quality of being steadfast; of hanging on despite the odds; of being dependable in any season. Love is the answer to how you need to conduct yourself in any circumstance. With love and faithfulness worn like priceless items of jewellery, you can go forth with confidence that you are on the right path. What's more, they will keep you from stumbling—holding you up like pillars—and shining like beacons in the dark. People will be drawn to your brilliance, and they will speak to each other of the sterling qualities of your character. To be a strong woman of courage all you need is love…and faithfulness!

JUNE 5

※

*And so we know and rely on the love God
has for us. God is love. Whoever lives in
love lives in God, and God in them.*

1 JOHN 4:16

Mother Teresa said, 'Spread love everywhere you go. Let
noone ever come to you without leaving happier'.
We're always looking for love and happiness. Today, girl,
you be the one to spread love and joy. The person who is
incapable of love is the one who feels unloved. But you are
truly loved by God. You live in His love; you float in it and
soak in it. Come alive to His love and then shower someone
else with it. Today, instead of focusing on your needs—which
are already met by God's love for you—think of someone else
who is in need of love, acceptance and happiness. One word
of kindness may be all someone requires to make their day. It
will also make your day to see someone smile because of you.

JUNE 6

❧

Be completely humble and gentle; be patient, bearing with one another in love.

EPHESIANS 4:2

If someone laughs at you…smile at them. Maybe their own insecurities are affecting their behaviour. You be the bigger person—because you are living in the light and love of God. Tell the person who is ridiculing you, that God loves her too—if not in words, then just by helping her feel better about herself—even if you aren't feeling your best. Perhaps all you're having is a bad hair day, but someone else may be having a bad relationship day, a bad finances day or a bad job day. As Maya Angelou said, *people will forget what you did, but they will never forget how you made them feel.*

JUNE 7

*For everything that was written in
the past was written to teach us, so
that through the endurance taught in
the Scriptures and the encouragement
they provide, we might have hope.*

ROMANS 15:4

Looking at everything that has to do with the present seems to strip us of all hope. Around us the world seems to be falling apart. It's strange to think that we need to go back to the past in order to find hope. The Reader's Digest once carried the story of a woman who was swimming in the ocean and was swept away from shore—so far that nobody could find her. As she struggled for days, suffering from extreme thirst, hunger and exhaustion, she managed to stay floating only because she kept herself conscious by feeding herself on happy memories. She drew on the past in order to keep herself afloat with hope in the present. Today, return to the word of God to give you hope not just for today but for tomorrow.

JUNE 8

Do not be slothful in zeal, be
fervent in spirit, serve the Lord.

ROMANS 12:11

When you don't particularly want to hang out with someone who is not your first choice when it comes to socialising, or when you are feeling inadequate because of how you perceive yourself and your abilities, remember that it's better to take one step in faith and see where it goes, than not to take a step at all and thus never know what might have been. It's the same with volunteering for an activity or an event, which places you at the center of a whole new experience or even an adventure. To serve in love is to serve God. It doesn't mean it has to be something big. It can be something small. If you can't make a wave, make a ripple. Eventually many ripples will form a wave.

JUNE 9

Behold, I have taken your iniquity away from you, and I will clothe you with pure vestments.

ZECHARIAH 3:4

Eleanour Roosevelt said that no one can make you feel inferior without your consent. Remember this when you're scrolling through Facebook or Instagram and wishing you were somebody else, living somewhere else, and enjoying what someone has erroneously led you to believe is…the life. Look into the mirror instead and and focus on what you have—the real life with a fresh start, every day. Your past mistakes obliterated, your painful choices forgotten, you embark each day on a fresh journey of discovery of who you truly are. What you discover will amaze, rather than distress, you. The new you will have new experiences and will not dwell in the failed past. The new you will not revert to old patterns because you will be forever changed from deep within. When God makes promises, He keeps them. So don your pure vestments and don't let anyone make you feel small, because girl, you are tall!

JUNE 10

***You were blameless in your ways
from the day you were created.***

EZEKIEL 28:15

So, you don't feel quite like that today because you have grown accustomed to pointing fingers at yourself. Self blame and self accusation can cripple you and make it hard for you to reach your full potential as a woman. Nora Ephron, the renowned filmmaker, said, '*Be the heroine of your life, not the victim*'. Funny (well not so funny actually) how a lot of women don't heed that advice. Today, remind yourself that you stand strong and true to who you are. Don't make excuses for why you are *you*. Aspire to be the best version of yourself, and remember that can only happen when you allow yourself to grow—unhampered by your own, or someone else's idea of what you should be.

JUNE 11

❧

Give me your heart,
and let your eyes observe my ways.

PROVERBS 23:26

It's a fact that you are influenced, and become like, the person you spend the most time with. Whatever you give your heart to, your mind becomes subject to. It can be your job, a lifestyle, or it can be God. Give Him you heart, and you will automatically desire to know more about Him. You will become hungry for knowledge of Him. You will, eventually, become a reflection of Him. Which is really what you should be, considering you are His child. This is the best version of yourself that you aspire to. Think about this today and may it help you with the decisions you are making for how you will spend your time, or what activities you will pursue. Let Him into your life and watch yourself transform.

JUNE 12

❧

You who seek God, let your hearts revive.

PSALM 69:32

Jackie Joyner-Kersee is regarded among the all-time greatest athletes in the heptathlon as well as the long jump. She said, *if I stop to kick every barking dog, I am not going to get where I am going.* She meant that if you allow every barbed remark aimed at you to slow you down or stop you in your tracks, you won't reach your goal. Stay determined not to allow your insecurities to get the better of you. People will always try to make you feel smaller than you are, but never tire of reminding yourself of who you are in God. He will revive your heart when you are flagging and faltering. Keep seeking His strength and you will keep going despite those who try to pull you down.

JUNE 13

❧

Be of good courage, and let us be
courageous for our people, and
for the cities of our God, and may
the Lord do what seems good to him.

2 SAMUEL 10:12

Madeleine Albright, the first female Secretary of State in US History, said something significant. She said, "It took me quite a long time to develop a voice, and now that I have it, I am not going to be silent." Women with the courage to speak up for themselves, and others, is something that this world badly needs at this time. Your voice is power. Your voice is going to shape a generation. The world needs to hear what you have to say. So, feed on the wisdom that God gives you and let it mould and shape your words, thoughts and deeds. Lady, you were born for such a time as this. Use your gentleness of spirit to advantage. Disarm the taunters with the sweetness of your voice.

JUNE 14

❧

And in the fourth watch of the night he came to them, walking on the sea. But when the disciples saw him walking on the sea, they were terrified, and said, "It is a ghost!" and they cried out in fear. But immediately Jesus spoke to them, saying, "Take heart; it is I. Do not be afraid."

MATTHEW 14:25-27

Fear is your enemy. Fear *is from* the enemy. The terrors of the night, the apprehensions of the day, the concerns and worries that limit your potential and age you ahead of time, are all a product of fear. Be of good courage. You may feel frail, but you are a woman, and you have steel and grit inside of you. You have what it takes to stand on top of the mountain and say, "I conquered this"! So even if that mountain is a pile of school work on an assignment… a difficult relationship, or a challenge you have accepted, take heart. While you are tackling the problem, God is transforming the situation… and in your most challenging hour, Jesus reaches out and says those words that calm your soul—"It is I. Do not be afraid."

JUNE 15

*And Peter answered him, "Lord, if it is you,
command me to come to you on the water." He
said, "Come." So Peter got out of the boat
and walked on the water and came to Jesus.*

MATTHEW 14:28-29

Amelia Earhart, the American aviation pioneer and author, said, 'the most difficult thing is the decision to act. The rest is merely tenacity." She was the first female aviator to fly solo across the Atlantic Ocean. Every day you are faced with an invitation to do something you haven't done before; to live life the way you never have before. Don't limit yourself by how you see yourself, but look at your potential as God views it. Peter was just a regular guy. There was nothing particularly extraordinary about him—except his tenacity. Even when he got it wrong, he kept going. Of all the disciples, it was Peter who walked on water and did it in the strength that he got from seeing his Master there before him. If you have the opportunity to step out of the boat today—to cross the boundaries of what's usual and do something incredible—go for it. You can do it!

JUNE 16

❧

But when he saw the wind, he was
afraid, and beginning to sink he
cried out, "Lord, save me."

MATTHEW 14: 30

On the other side of a bold decision is the fear of sinking. But you know that fear is from the enemy. It's a lie that makes you think you need to keep anticipating that everything is going to collapse around you. Oprah Winfrey, the famous talk show host, says, "Step out of the history that is holding you back. Step into the new story you are willing to create." Yesterday we looked at Peter stepping out and walking on water. Today we look at the fear that gripped him when he realised he had had the courage to step out of the boat. Yes, a bold decision may keep you up at night wondering if you've taken leave of your senses. Turn over and go to sleep knowing that the only thing you took leave of was the false security of doing the usual thing. Why would God fill you with so much potential if he wanted you to stay in the same groove you've been in for all of your life this far?

JUNE 17

◦⁓◦

Jesus immediately reached out his hand and took hold of him, saying to him, "O you of little faith, why did you doubt?"

MATTHEW 14:31

The only time you falter, or sink, is when you allow fear to turn into doubt, and doubt to escalate into the monster that threatens to drown you. Submerged in a sea of fear and doubt you struggle and cry out, but your heavenly father is still by your side, reaching out and asking you, with tenderness, and just a tinge of impatience—'Daughter, why can't you learn how to trust me? I am not like the other people in your life. I will never let you down. Place your hand in mine and keep going. We're going to be doing so much more than just walking on water. In fact, my beautiful child, we're going to transform the world together. Yes, it will mean taking the boat a little further out, but when you do that, you will discover just what I can do through you!'

JUNE 18

❧

But we have this treasure in jars of clay, to show that the surpassing power belongs to God and not to us.

2 CORINTHIANS 4:7

Today is the first day of the rest of your life. Discover the potential that you haven't explored yet. Step out of your comfort zone and see where the winds of change and transformation take you. Learn something new. Open your mind and heart to an experience you have never had before. Try a new flavour of ice-cream. Don't order the same takeaway you have been ordering every week. Savour life. Don't miss the sunset—paint it. Don't ignore an emotion you feel—write about it. Don't fail to capture a moment in the lyrics of a song that flows from your pen. Take your eyes off your mobile phone and look into the faces of people around you. Smile at someone. Say a kind word to another. God within you is yearning to make a difference through you. He gave you life. His power wells up from within you. Don't waste it. Discover it…beginning from this moment.

JUNE 19

~

*O Lord, you have searched me and known
me! You know when I sit down and when I
rise up; you discern my thoughts from afar.*

PSALM 139:1-2

How great it is that you are known by God. Mother
Teresa said, "*Every human being has a longing for
God. Not only do we long for God, but we have the treasure of
His presence always with us.*" Hold this thought close when
someone says something about you that you know isn't true.
Rather than retaliate, reassure yourself that God knows you.
He has searched you. He is with you. He even knows what
you're thinking right at this moment. He created you with
love and He created you to be loved. So go out there and
be the amazing, loving, lovable person that you were made
to be. Don't let anyone make you feel like you don't matter,
because you do matter—every hair on your head is precious
and counted.

JUNE 20

❧

Where shall I go from your Spirit?
Or where shall I flee from your presence?

PSALM 139:7-8

'You can run but you can't hide'. Well, that's not a threat but rather an assurance that you are always within God's view. He is watching over you, so much so that He anticipates your every need. He wakes you up in the morning, when you are about to oversleep and miss your bus to school or your ride to work. He calms your fears because He can see all your thoughts—every dream, doubt or fear. There are moments when you may feel isolated. You suffer a setback of sorts and don't particularly feel like being social. You cut yourself off from even your very best friend. You even cut yourself off from God and wonder if He is there at all. All the while that you think you're far away from Him, He is drawing closer and trying to speak to you. Today, listen to His voice. It's the force of Life that lifts you up and sets you on your feet again.

JUNE 21

But the one who endures to
the end will be saved.

MATTHEW 10:22

It's not winning the race that matters but running it. Life is never about how much you achieve, but how many lives you touch along the way. It's not the exam you sit for, but the knowledge you acquire in preparing for it. Endurance is not sitting there and letting life happen. It's going out there and making every moment count. It's learning from every mile of the marathon and deriving value from it. Today, don't settle for anything less than a life that challenges you, and a future that unveils your potential. It's only when you run the first mile that you know what it takes to cover the distance. And that spurs you on for the next mile and the next. You will only know who you truly are when your endurance is put to the test. You can do it. You were made to endure!

JUNE 22

For this reason I remind you to fan into flame the gift of God, which is in you.

2 TIMOTHY 1:6

Maya Angelou said, "My mission in life is not merely to survive, but to thrive!" To truly live your life there cannot be an absence of action. Real living is taking a step out of your comfort zone and striking out. It is getting out there, running the race with passion and zeal; taking the blows as they come and continuing to go with the torch still burning. To live is not to burn the candle at both ends and burn out. It is fanning into flame the potential and passion within yourself and making things happen that you never believed were possible. To survive is passive. To thrive is active. Take the active route today. Reassess your life and give yourself the opportunity to really discover what you are made of. There's a lot within you that you will never know about until you take it out for a test drive.

JUNE 23

◦⁓◦

*Therefore, my beloved brothers, be
steadfast, immovable, always abounding
in the work of the Lord, knowing that
in the Lord your labor is not in vain.*

1 CORINTHIANS 15:58

Helen Keller said, "*When we do the best we can, we never
know what miracle is wrought in our life, or in the life of
another.*" She was born deaf and blind, yet she made a mark
on the world. Simply by doing her best. Today, even if you
feel you aren't succeeding in what you have set out to do,
keep going. Persevere, and remain steadfast. You will reach
your goal eventually. Nothing that you do with the best of
intentions is ever in vain. It's a win-win situation each time
you make an effort. The rewards may not always be visible,
but they are there. You are inspiring somebody else just by
what you are persistently and consistently doing. God sees
your efforts and the prize that comes from Him is more than
all the acclaim you get from the world.

JUNE 24

❧

*If we confess our sins, he is faithful
and just to forgive us our sins and to
cleanse us from all unrighteousness.*

1 JOHN 1:9

We do the laundry faithfully. We wash the dishes and take the trash out. We vacuum and dust. We rake the leaves and sweep the yard. Why then is it so difficult to acknowledge that there may be litter that has to be dealt with in the recesses of our hearts and minds? Thoughts we shouldn't entertain or actions that are questionable; words that were said that maybe caused someone pain? What do we do with all that? The fact is, if you leave it untended, it will choke you. It will weigh you down. You will cease to function with ease—like a garden that isn't being tended gets choked with weeds, or a pool that isn't cleaned gets filled with grime. Today, follow a simple process to give your mind, heart and soul a thorough cleaning. Just talk to your heavenly father and tell him what you know is inside of you that you're not happy with. He will take it all away and replace the clutter with His peace.

JUNE 25

⁓

*You shall not covet your neighbor's
house; you shall not covet your neighbor's
wife, or his male servant, or his female
servant, or his ox, or his donkey, or
anything that is your neighbor's.*

EXODUS 20:17

When you're scrolling through Instagram or Facebook and see that one friend is enjoying a vacation in Greece, while another has bought a new car and the third has somehow managed to get the body of a Victoria's Secret model, try not to go green with envy. Covetiousness is toxic to your system. It does strange things to your behaviour and if you entertain it, it will take you over and turn you into someone you wouldn't like to be! Stop that from happening right now. If you can't stay away from social media, then do this—each time you see your friends achieving, or doing, or enjoying something you can't, say thank you to God for all that you have. There's power in praise. Go over all that you should be grateful for in your life. You will find yourself feeling buoyed up once again.

JUNE 26

❧

For by the grace given to me I say to everyone among you not to think of himself more highly than he ought to think, but to think with sober judgment, each according to the measure of faith that God has assigned.

ROMANS 12:3

Jesse Jackson said, "*Never look down on anybody, unless you're helping them up.*" Oprah Winfrey said that the best way to succeed is to discover what you love and then find a way to offer it to others in the form of service. To help and serve are key to living a fulfilling life. Remember that when success may tempt you to think that someone else may be less capable or gifted than you are. Today, try and get to know a person before you make any hasty assessments about them. Discover their hidden qualities. Uncover the treasure which they have in some measure. Find ways to do something for someone. Believe in the potential of everyone. Be inspired and be an inspiration. Everybody is a winner. Everybody has something to recommend them. Encourage someone who is feeling small, to walk tall. The more you do that, the bigger your life will become.

JUNE 27

And we know that for those who love God all things work together for good, for those who are called according to his purpose.

ROMANS 8:28

To be like a piece of driftwood on the waves might have echoes of freedom, but when you think about it, that piece of driftwood is going nowhere. It serves no meaningful purpose. Today, seek your purpose and plan your path—with God's help of course. John F. Kennedy said, "*Efforts and courage are not enough without purpose and direction.*" And all effort is fruitless if not firmly embedded in the will and purpose of God. You have an important purpose to your life. Do everything in your power to discover exactly what it is. When you do, plan to pursue it to the best of your ability. God will give you direction if you would only ask for it. Trying to steer the course of your life by yourself is like trying to navigate the seas without a rudder. Be wise. Take instruction and succeed in reaching your goals successfully.

JUNE 28

❧

Why are you cast down, O my soul,
and why are you in turmoil within
me? Hope in God; for I shall again
praise him, my salvation.

PSALM 42:5

It's normal to feel downcast occasionally, but it's important not to let that escalate into depression. Depression exists where hope has taken flight. Hold on to the promises of God. Speak them into your life every day and keep the clouds of gloom away. After all, you're young and your life is full of promise. You have everything going for you. Even though you may have suffered a major disappointment, choose to hold on to hope for all you're worth. Christopher Reeve said, *"Once you choose hope, anything's possible."* Hope is knowing that God has a plan for your welfare and that He is working to fulfill that plan. He will never leave you nor forsake you. So have a good cry, but after you've dried your tears, put some music on and dance your blues away. Tomorrow, the sun will shine again.

JUNE 29

I am the vine; you are the branches.
Whoever abides in me and I in him,
he it is that bears much fruit, for
apart from me you can do nothing.

JOHN 15:5

There's something comforting about knowing that we are not walking this road alone. Having your circle of friends or your gal pals as a support group gives you the strength you need to go from day to day. Yet these human sources of strength often give way and let you down. Not so your father God. He will never fail you. Cast your burden upon Him. Tune in every day. His comfort is like a warm blanket on a winter's night—it's soothing and protective. It is always there to draw on. Like a branch is nothing when severed from the vine, we cease to function at our full potential when we are distanced from our Maker. Today, reconnect and be revived. You need to be revived to survive.

JUNE 30

*I, I am he who blots out your
transgressions for my own sake, and
I will not remember your sins.*

ISAIAH 43:25

Think about this. From this moment on, you walk away with a clean slate. And you are once again feeling on top of the world. This is freedom. The liberty to live life without the burden of past mistakes. Let's face it, everybody messes up at some point. Everyone has a past. But today you are given the opportunity to draw the curtains across that past and when you look in the rear-view mirror, all you see is a pristine landscape—untouched, unspoilt. It is the gift that God gives you because He loves you. Don't toss it away for a lifetime of self-destructive self pity. Self-pity has no friends, whereas freedom is always popular. What you hold on to and what you let go of, will determine the course of your life from now on.

NOTES

_____

_____

_____

_____

_____

_____

_____

_____

_____

_____

_____

_____

JULY

JULY 1

*I will give peace in the land, and you shall
lie down, and none shall make you afraid.*

LEVITICUS 26:6

There may be times when you wonder if it's okay to step
outside the safety of your comfort zone. But if you want
to discover your true potential, then even if the waters may
look intimidating, it's time to step out of the boat. Girl, you
are made of sterner stuff than you ever imagined. So, go out
there and show them what you're made of. A daughter of
God owns the world. Go out there and own it! Stake your
claim on the future you were called upon to take charge
of. That school you want to apply to… or that job you are
wondering if you should aim for—go for it!

JULY 2

*For as high as the heavens are above
the earth, so great is his steadfast
love toward those who fear him.*

PSALM 103:11

In a world of uncertainty, one thing remains certain—that if you seek the love and peace of God, you will stand firm. Woman, stay strong in that quiet confidence that you are dear to Him who called you into this world for a purpose. Turn away from situations or people who tell you otherwise. You are significant, even if it sometimes feels like you are getting lost in the crowd. Discovering your ability to shine despite the odds, is the greatest accomplishment. And it all begins with making up your mind to go fearlessly forward because the Only One you need to fear is the source of your courage.

JULY 3

❧

As far as the east is from the west, so far
does he remove our transgressions from us.

PSALM 103:12

Another day, another goof up. Sounds familiar? Well, who hasn't been there? The thing about making a mess of things is that you get to discover what not to do the next time around. And there will be an opportunity to get it right. So don't waste any tears on what went wrong… but stay determined to figure out how to avoid a similar situation next time around. Oscar Wilde said, 'experience is simply the name we give our mistakes'. So, the next time you take that map out and begin to drive, it's okay if you wind up at the opposite end of your destination. Who knows, perhaps you were actually meant to be there at that moment in time. Get the most out of the experience of being somewhere that you weren't intending to be. Life, ultimately, is what you make of it.

JULY 4

*Blessed is the one who does not
walk in step with the wicked.*

PSALM 1:1

Who are you trying to keep pace with? With who, or what, are you measuring your achievements or accomplishments? The fact is, you are wired differently from everyone else. You are uniquely made to go at a certain pace and be good at certain things. So, push yourself towards positive goals, and steer clear of a negative mindset. You were born from light and made to shine. But you can only shine if you draw upon your own strengths and abilities and not measure yourself by anyone else's standards. Maybe that lifestyle that you're trying to adopt is not meant for you. Maybe you are desperately flapping your wings against the bars of that particular cage and wanting to be set free. Be who you were born to be. Be you!

JULY 5

❧

Like a tree planted by streams of water,
which yields its fruit in season
and whose leaf does not wither—
whatever they do prospers.

PSALM 1:3

Today, as the first shaft of sunlight drifts onto your pillow, let it caress your face and awaken you to a new reality. You have potential. You are fruitful. You will prosper. Wipe the sleep from your eyes and look ahead with greater clarity. Today is a new day with new hope, and every moment is filled with new possibilities. Yield yourself to the promise held in this shaft of sunlight and allow your spirits to soar. Stretch, luxuriate, and set yourself free from every negative thought that's holding you back. The key to success is to stand in front of a closed door and yet see everything that lies behind and beyond it.

JULY 6

❧

Today I have become your father.
Ask me, and I will make the
nations your inheritance, the ends
of the earth your possession.

PSALM 2:7-8

It's time to take hold of the promises made to you as a child of God instead of feeling like you don't deserve to enjoy everything that you have a right to. This world, and everything in it, is yours. So, keep dreaming, and making plans, because your heavenly dad is just waiting to show you all of His beautiful creation. Start first with discovering your own neighbourhood. Meet the people there and exchange smiles. You'll feel your heart begin to swell with joy and hope. Reach out to someone who needs a word of comfort. Give somebody a hug. Draw from the strengths that are inherent to your nature as a woman.

JULY 7

~·~

Blessed are all who take refuge in him.

PSALM 2:12

I magine a bank that you can draw from anytime, all the time. Imagine a power source that you can plug into anytime, all the time. Helen Keller said, '*Faith is the strength by which a shattered world shall emerge into light.*" You can draw on the strength of God and His power, and literally see the world light up around you. *Taking refuge* isn't running away or going into hiding. It's seeking shelter in the midst of a storm—or just recuperating or replenishing your stores of energy and strength. Today, seek refuge in Him before you even begin your day. You will feel your mind ready, refreshed, and prepared to take on just about anything!

JULY 8

❦

But you, Lord, are a shield around me,
my glory, the One who lifts my head high.

PSALM 3:3

When you're not feeling particularly in control, it's worth remembering that you have a shield around you. That shield is literally a wall of protection—within which you can be vulnerable and expose your true self. When you acknowledge the reality of who you are—strengths, weaknesses and everything else—and accept that this is *you*, you will feel so much better. So often we are tempted to hide behind an image of who we think we ought to be instead of being who we really are. If you relate to this, then remember you have a shield, a fortress, within which you are strong no matter how you perceive yourself or your abilities. Hold your head high. Walk in His glory.

JULY 9

❧

I call out to the Lord,
and he answers me from his holy mountain.

PSALM 3:4

How often when you just need someone to be there for you, you have a list of contacts but don't know who to call. You may even dial someone's number and hang up… and then send them a text saying you called by mistake. And then, you feel like you're losing control and there's nobody to help you keep it together. Sounds familiar? Author and Journalist, Germany Kent, said, '*Where God guides, He provides. No matter how things look, God is still in control.*' So even though you may sometimes feel like you're unravelling, or your nerves are on edge, or you're just not ready to take on the challenge that's ahead of you—*don't panic.* You don't even have to be in control, because He is. Surrender to His care. It's all you need to succeed.

JULY 10

❧

I lie down and sleep;
I wake again, because the Lord sustains me.

PSALM 3:5

There is such a sense of comfort in knowing that even while you sleep you are being watched over. The seed sleeps in the soil in the certainty that it will wake up as a plant. The unborn baby sleeps in its mother's womb with the confidence that it will wake in her arms. You lie beneath a blanket of the Father's love which rejuvenates you during those hours of rest. Bill Johnson said, '*You have authority over every storm you can sleep in.*' While you're awake, you're at work and you can't help trying to solve your own problems, even if you're not doing the best job of it. While you sleep, God's at work. The next time you have a problem, sleep over it—let Him take charge!

JULY 11

*I will not fear though tens of thousands
assail me on every side.*

PSALM 3:6

The thing about being a young adult is that you're on the cusp. You're getting to adulthood, but you're not there yet. You're still figuring out things, and life can sometimes get a bit too much to handle. Your biggest problem at this time might be dealing with people who are all in the same boat as you are. Everyone is struggling to be understood and even to understand themselves. There seems to be conflict around every corner, and there may be times when you feel almost fearful to take the next step because you don't know what you will encounter. The future is shrouded in mystery and so are you. You are still discovering yourself. Plato said, *'Courage is knowing what not to fear'*. Don't fear tomorrow and don't fear yourself. God knows how both are going to turn out and He has everything under control.

JULY 12

❧

From the Lord comes deliverance.

PSALM 3:8

There are some decisions that can only be implemented at the other end of a conversation or a telephone call. Ending a relationship that was hurting you…or finally having an honest conversation with someone to sort out a misunderstanding. These things can keep you up at night—tossing till the wee hours; irresolute and troubled over the consequences. *But you like him*—though he's taking advantage of you. *But you can't tell him what you really feel.* Hiding behind the 'can't' is like being shackled. You need deliverance. You need to make a decision. Your peace of mind depends on it.

JULY 13

*Know that the Lord has set apart
his faithful servant for himself.*

PSALM 4:3.

There's joy in knowing that you were created for a purpose. This is a truth that many search for through a major part of their lives. There is an even greater sense of happiness in knowing that you have been *set apart* for God for His purpose. That doesn't mean that you're above anyone or need to keep away from everyone. It just means that you have been chosen to play a significant role in this life and that everything you do will therefore have meaning. You can happily wake up to that realisation everyday! So what do you do? Just be good to everyone around you. Look outward rather than just dwelling on your own wellbeing. Think about someone else and do something, however small, to make someone else feel special.

JULY 14

❦

In peace I will lie down and sleep, for you alone, Lord, make me dwell in safety.

PSALM 4:8

Sleep is important, yet the world does everything possible to rob you of it. Put aside your mobile phone, tablet and any other device, and surrender to rest and repose. Let yourself be enfolded in a cocoon of tranquility where you feel safe, protected and completely loved. Restful sleep is devoid of nightmares and disturbing dreams. Empty your mind of worry and let stress float away on a golden cloud of total peace. And at the other end of this blissful rest, awaken to a joyful dawn and the start of another day where you are refreshed and ready to take on the world. Give sleep a priority if you want to go through the day like the winner you are!

JULY 15

❦

But let all who take refuge in you be glad;
let them ever sing for joy. Spread your
protection over them, that those who
love your name may rejoice in you.

PSALM 5:11

When life gets too much for you to handle, and there are challenges or difficulties of one kind or another, what will you take solace or refuge in? Will it be in a habit or addiction; a detrimental relationship or a friendship that leads you astray? Or will you call upon Him in your day of trouble and have your heavenly father come to your rescue? Nestle under His blanket of protection—it will keep you sheltered and safe. His name is sweet and His presence is sweeter. Today, tell someone about the nurturing, protective love of the Father. Tell them that everyone is welcome under the blanket of His divine protection.

JULY 16

My shield is God Most High,
who saves the upright in heart.

PSALM 7:10

We all face arrows everyday. They can be in the form of unkind words, anger, unfair attitudes, or just the apathy of people. Imagine holding out a shield to catch every poisoned arrow, fiery dart or missile. And then imagine that this shield that you hold out is the name of your Heavenly Father. The moment you cry out to Him, He takes the blows, arrows and darts on your behalf and deflects them so that you are not hurt. What's more, He comforts and reassures you that the people aiming those arrows didn't really know what they were doing. They acted in ignorance…and He helps you forgive them. What a joy to live right, feel right and just be alright because you are shielded.

JULY 17

～&

*The fear of the Lord is the beginning
of knowledge: but fools despise
wisdom and instruction.*

PROVERBS 1:7

So, you tried to advise your friend who asked you what you thought about something or someone, and instead of being grateful, she actually showed you the door. Now you feel dreadful about the whole situation. This wasn't how it was meant to turn out. You beat yourself up. You wonder if you should have put things differently or not spoken up at all. You know what you said was absolutely true and correct, and you gave her the wisdom she needed to deal with something—but she decided not to heed your advice. Don't worry. You did your best and your intentions were pure. Now let your friend ruminate a bit over what you said. She will soon be back saying you were right…but sometimes the truth hurts.

JULY 18

❧

Out in the open wisdom calls aloud,
she raises her voice in the public square;
on top of the wall she cries out, at
the city gate she makes her speech.

PROVERBS 1:21

There's a time to be silent and a time to speak out. Injustice is everywhere. Abuse is rife. How long will people turn the other way and pretend they can't see what's going on? You, beautiful woman, are strong. You are a conqueror. You are a leader. On you rests the onus to speak up and speak out. Take up the cause of the underdog. Speak for the persecuted—the person who gets picked on and ridiculed; the co-worker who keeps getting passed over for a promotion. Elevate people and God will elevate you. Reach out your hand to help someone up and God will raise you up. Don't be afraid to voice your opinions when they are based on a just viewpoint. Stand with the God of Justice to fight injustice today.

JULY 19

❧

I will pour out my thoughts to you,
I will make known to you my teachings.

PROVERBS 1:23

Socrates said, '*the only true wisdom is in knowing you know nothing*'. There's a certain advantage to knowing nothing, and that is because the people who think they know everything, end up not learing anything at all. To be empty is to have the capacity to be filled. Which is not to say that you need to profess to be without all knowledge. No. You do have knowledge and wisdom. But to allow yourself to feel that you are empty and need to be filled is to open yourself up to receive. True leaders are teachable. The know-it-all never grows or evolves. Woman, you are wise, and the wise know how to gain more wisdom. Open your mind and receive that which is being promised to you by the Repository of All Wisdom.

JULY 20

❧

But whoever listens to me will live in safety
and be at ease, without fear of harm.

PROVERBS 1:33

William Shakespeare said, '*The fool doth think he is wise, but the wise man knows himself to be a fool*'. This is a humbling thought. Especially since we desperately want to believe we are the ultimate authority on our lives. So we lash out at well meaning friends, family members and people in authority. Some even think they don't need the wisdom that comes from God himself. Listen, learn and be safe. You are precious to your Heavenly Father and He wants the best for you. Open your mind and heart to the instruction He is giving you. He loves His little girl and wants her to be safe. You will hear His voice like a little nudge or a whisper that people call intuition or instinct. Be wise, take note, listen!

JULY 21

~⁓

If you call out for insight and cry aloud for understanding, and if you look for it as for silver and search for it as for hidden treasure, then you will understand the fear of the Lord and find the knowledge of God.

PROVERBS 2:3-5

A walk on the beach at night—with the sound of the waves in your ears, and the surf illuminated by the moonlight—evokes such emotion. The sand slipping between your toes, the breeze in your hair—what powerful sensations. You feel alive amidst the beauty of nature. You don't want to pause, rewind or fast forward. You are completely in the moment. If only you could approach all of life like this— savouring every tiny moment and magnifying it into a memory that you want to cling on to forever—how precious every day would be. Today, girl, may you have the insight and understanding to stop and look up at the sky and feel the joy of riding on a cloud…if only in your imagination.

JULY 22

Discretion will protect you,
and understanding will guard you.

PROVERBS 2:11

I n the careful choice of words lies peace, harmony and understanding. But if you were always to be weighing out and measuring your words before you spoke them, you would probably have to go through life tongue-tied. However, it is wise to remember that hasty words hurt and putting your foot in your mouth causes a great deal of discomfort—literally. A wise man once said, '*You can change the course of your life with your words*'. Really? But how will you know which words alter your life positively and which have a negative impact? You can speak wisdom to someone you care about and cause offense. Understanding what to say, and when to say it, is key. This is called *Discretion*.

JULY 23

❧

Wisdom will save you from the ways
of wicked men, from men whose
words are perverse, who have left the
straight paths to walk in dark ways.

PROVERBS 2: 12-13

There are all sorts of people out there, and the world is not always a safe place. If you're thinking of venturing out alone, whether in the physical realm or the virtual, exercise caution. Girl, you're precious, and though you are strong, you are also vulnerable. Don't let yourself be swayed by honeyed words sliding off a glib tongue, because you may just get trapped in a sticky mess. Wisdom is the ability to discern which situations are positive and which are to be avoided. Wisdom helps you steer clear of circumstances that are non-conducive to your safety and wellbeing. Wisdom is like a lamp that shines in the darkness and sheds light on schemes and traps. Outside of the shadows is a world that's safe and enjoyable. Be wise—stay in the light.

JULY 24

❧

Go to the ant,
consider its ways and be wise!
It has no commander, no overseer or ruler,
yet it stores its provisions in summer
and gathers its food at harvest.

PROVERBS 6:6-8

Thornton T. Munger said, '*The habit of saving is itself an education; it fosters every virtue, teaches self-denial, cultivates the sense of order, trains to forethought, and so broadens the mind.*' Saving is crucial. It is an art that involves not being tight-fisted, but exercising discretion when it comes to spending. Putting something by for a rainy day is the essence of saving. The fable of the ant and the grasshopper comes to mind when you think of letting money slip through your fingers. The fact is, there is temptation all around us to spend on things we don't need. The Internet has opened up a wealth of possibilities to lose wealth quite systematically and consistently. Woman, you need to be self sufficient. Be generous but don't be a spendthrift. In your genes lies the ability to stretch a dollar. Save as you stretch your finances.

JULY 25

Now then, my children, listen to me;
blessed are those who keep my ways.
Listen to my instruction and be wise.

PROVERBS 8:32-33

So, you finally think you've got things together. You're in control now. You've sorted things out. You've untied the knots. Now you can relax. You're singing '*I did it my way*' and you've never felt stronger. And then—ever so subtly that you barely notice until it creeps up on you—everything unravels, and the control you thought you were exercising now has a hold on you and it won't let go. And then your phone rings. And it's one of your parents, an elder sibling, or a mentor… and you don't want to hear the words '*I told you so*', so you ignore the call. It's okay, you think to yourself, I'll just get myself together again and keep going. But just as you're beginning to unravel again, stop and hear the voice that's telling you that you don't need to be in control because He is. Listen to what He has to say, because His words bring life.

JULY 26

❧

The righteous will never be uprooted.

PROVERBS 10:30

Life's storms are bad, but life's hurricanes are sometimes intolerable. Except this time, you're not falling apart because you have your life on track. You are unshakeable, because you are rooted in faith and grounded in wisdom. You have submitted and surrendered the outcome of things to The Lord, and you are assured of His love, provision and strength when the storm hits or the hurricane strikes. Nothing can shake you. Nothing can cause you to falter. Your strength is in Him now. You know you can rely on Him and He will never let you down. So that's what your belief is rooted in—the firm assurance that no matter what hits you, you will not fall. Keep strong girl, you're a winner.

JULY 27

❧

From the mouth of the righteous
comes the fruit of wisdom.

Remember when you needed advice and you didn't know who to get it from? Do you recall that when you did ask somebody to help you out with a solution to a problem, it just made things worse? But you have gained wisdom. You are growing and evolving. You have experience that has equipped you to counsel someone who needs it. Reach out today and help someone with a word of encouragement or advice. Sure, you're young, but you're growing. As you grow and learn, give some of that learning away to someone, and you will be making place to learn some more. As you give, so will you get. In fact, the more you give, the more you will receive.

JULY 28

A kindhearted woman gains honour.

PROVERBS 11:16

In a world where everyone is looking out for themselves, you be the kind woman who looks out for someone else. Start with something small, like calling someone who is lonely, and including them in an activity that you plan. Maybe invite someone for coffee, or cook a meal for somebody who's not doing too well, and take it across to their home. The heart of a woman was made to love, care and nurture. It is a reflection of God's own heart for people. Find your true personality in a deed of kindness—not something that's forced or contrived but that comes naturally to you, oh woman who cares!

JULY 29

∿

A generous person will prosper;
whoever refreshes others will be refreshed.

PROVERBS 11:25

A river flows, and on either side of its banks sprout up plants and trees. In the trees, birds make their nests and under the branches people find shade to rest. Animals come to drink from the river. The farmer uses the water to irrigate his fields. The more the river gives, the more it is loved and the more it receives. The rain replenishes it, and God's own hand is on it, as it abounds in every manner of goodness. Fish swim in its depths. Children run along the banks and play in the shade. Woman, be like the river. Your role in the community is significant and much needed. You bring value to every neighbourhood when you give of yourself and your resources.

JULY 30

*Those who know your name trust
in you, for you, Lord, have never
forsaken those who seek you.*

PSALM 9:10

It's comforting to know that you can go through life secure in the knowledge that you will never be alone. That you will always have the reserves of strength that you need. Even if your friends forsake you or your loved ones desert you, you know you have The Lord on your side. He is impartial. He loves unconditionally. He does not judge you. He showers you with His grace and love. You are eternally provided for, eternally blessed, eternally loved. What an incredible realisation to wake up to each day. What a source of strength. It's like having a well to draw from every moment of every day…and a pair of strong arms to hold you when you are tired and need to rest.

JULY 31

I will give thanks to you, Lord, with all my heart; I will tell of all your wonderful deeds. I will be glad and rejoice in you; I will sing the praises of your name, O Most High.

PSALM 9:1-2

Today, give thanks to The Lord for all that He has done for you—not with mere words or even a song, but with the deeds He loves to bless. Tell someone about His loving kindness. Reassure a stranger that she is not alone. Take a walk today. Look around you at creation. Imagine what it might have been like on that first day when everything was made, and the animals and birds were placed on the earth. Lift up your heart in gratitude for the air you breathe, and the firm ground you walk on. Discover the words within yourself to express what you are feeling at this moment in time. Unlock more of your potential. Unleash a talent or skill. Believe in it. Believe in you.

NOTES

_____

_____

_____

_____

_____

_____

_____

_____

_____

_____

_____

_____

_____

AUGUST

AUGUST 1

❧

Think how you have instructed many,
how you have strengthened feeble hands.

JOB 4:3

When your spirits are flagging, and you just don't feel your usual happy self, remind yourself of others to whom you showed kindness; people you encouraged with just a few simple words or a smile that came from your heart. Now use that as a fountain of joy that you can come to and drink from. You have a lot to give, because you have a good heart. It might not always be easy to put a smile on your own face, but it sure gets easier when you put a smile on someone else's face first. Joel Osteen said, '*When things are difficult, smile by faith. Don't wait until you feel better*'.

AUGUST 2

❧

Your words have supported those who stumbled; you have strengthened faltering knees.

JOB 4:4

The power of words cannot be underestimated. They either build up or tear down. A few well-chosen words can make you feel like a million bucks. That's why you need to weigh and measure them—especially when you know that they may be influenced by your mood. Some people always know the right thing to say. Others just wish they could take back their words the moment they are out. When you are at a loss for words, or don't know how to quell a flood of angry words, lean into The Word of all words and remember how He cares for those who stumble—yes, even those who stumble on their words. You will feel renewed strength. In fact, the more you connect with The Word, the more you will be empowered to use words more effectively.

AUGUST 3

~

He performs wonders that cannot be fathomed, miracles that cannot be counted.

JOB 5:9

The situation seems irredeemable. You feel like you've come to the end of your resources. You have nothing more to give. Maybe it's an exam that didn't go well or an application that wasn't accepted. Or maybe it's just something that you've been striving for and hoping against hope will unfold in just the way that you want it to. Well, it's time to step back and let Him take over. You will be amazed at how situations can be turned around—even the most impossible of them all. Give your Heavenly Father a chance to demonstrate His love for you.

AUGUST 4

❧

He provides rain for the earth;
he sends water on the countryside.

JOB 5:10

Almost everyone you meet is waiting for a dream to come true or a miracle to happen. This phase of your life, and every season after that, brings miracles wrapped up in challenges. It would be great if things happened at the snap of your fingers, but perhaps it's better this way because you will savour the rewards all the more. Use the time of waiting to strengthen your faith muscles. Pray—for your own needs and for others. Never cease hoping. Always make time to enjoy the gifts of Nature—the breathtaking sunrises and sunsets. Relish every meal you have. Take time to appreciate the goodness of what comes from the earth. You will feel your perspective shift as you wait. And maybe your dreams will change too. Maybe you will realise that what you need is what you had all along.

AUGUST 5

❧

You will be protected from the lash of the tongue, and need not fear when destruction comes.

JOB 5:21

Like trees and plants are pruned and cut back for stronger growth, there are things in your life that need to be to be cut out or cut back in order for you to grow. Those friends who think they're doing you a world of good by chipping away at your self esteem; those situations in which you frequently find yourself, that make you question your significance on this planet; even those places you feel you need to go to in order to feel like you're with it…assess their relevance in your life. You might just discover that you've outgrown some stuff, or else your growth is being severely curbed just by holding on to some things. Take a good hard look at what you've been settling for. Walk away from the tongue lashers and the destructive influences. It's time for a new way of life!

AUGUST 6

❧

Oh, that I might have my request,
that God would grant what I hope for.

JOB 6:8

Summer is still here. The warmth of the sun, the laughter of friends, and time to sit back and just be. If you're making this season all about getting things done and packing as much activity into each day, then you need to rethink what you regard as leisure. Give yourself time to dream, to think of what could be. Listen to the wind in the trees. Or even the sounds of traffic. Allow yourself to luxuriate in the reality of who you are. Get in touch with *you*! How long have you been away from yourself while you were chasing deadlines and dealing with the hectic pace of life? Yes, summer is here. Don't look beyond it. For now…just enjoy the moment.

AUGUST 7

❧

*He will yet fill your mouth with laughter
and your lips with shouts of joy.*

JOB 8:21

Somehow, life has become all about chasing dreams—sometimes impossible ones. Often, as you chase a dream, you lose your vision. Blinded by what you so desperately seek, you forget to see what lies immediately before you. And so, you lose out on today, in your frenetic quest for tomorrow. Woman, you don't have to prove anything to anyone. You just need to be the best version of yourself, and to do that you need to slow down and get in touch with the real you. Connect with the essence of who you are. This is how you can move forward with greater confidence in your ability to achieve the impossible.

AUGUST 8

~❧~

*You gave me life and showed me kindness, and
in your providence watched over my spirit.*

JOB 10:12

Today, think of the moment when you were born.
The ecstatic welcome by your parents and the people
standing by. Your first cry, and all the milestones that your
parents celebrated as you grew up. The fact is, they never
stopped celebrating your birth. Neither did heaven. Everyday,
every moment, you are lovingly watched over, and all your
achievements get a collective shout of applause. You are also
watched when you're not quite getting to where you want to,
and your efforts are applauded, nonetheless. Today, ease up
on yourelf gorgeous girl, and cut yourself some slack. Take
your time. You will get there. This isn't a race. It's life. And
you were made to enjoy it.

AUGUST 9

You will lift up your face; you will stand firm and without fear.

JOB 11:15

Henry Ford said, '*One of the greatest discoveries a man makes, one of his greatest surprises, is to find he can do what he was afraid he couldn't do.*" Wow! Just think about it! That speech you were asked to give and you refused because you didn't think you could; that play you were asked to take part in, and you said no because you were afraid you would get stage fright…or that commitment you were asked to make but you backed away because you were afraid you wouldn't be able to live up to someone's expectations…they're all easily done if you would but take a single step towards doing them. Don't miss out on the best part of your life simply because you are afraid. You are a woman. A courageous woman. You can do it. You just need to believe that you can.

AUGUST 10

❧

You will surely forget your trouble,
recalling it only as waters gone by.
Life will be brighter than noonday,
and darkness will become like morning.

JOB 11:16-17

When life throws you lemons, make yourself a glass of lemonade and read the promises made by your Heavenly Father. Between the pages of the greatest Book ever written, lie treasures that will add value to your life; illuminating thoughts that will light up your world; incredible truths that will feed your soul. Yes, life is meant to be enjoyed. You were meant to live it to its fullest. When you uncover the truth and the treasure, you will also find revealed the secrets to how you can release the potential to be everything you were meant to be. You will then begin to live. Truly live!

AUGUST 11

*You will be secure, because there is hope;
you will look about you and take
your rest in safety. You will lie down,
with no one to make you afraid…*

JOB 11:18-19

Have you ever strung a hammock up between two trees and lain there with a book, with the sunlight filtering through the leaves casting patterns on your face? Through light and shadow, shapes emerge. They form a story—the fruit of your imagination. You lay the book aside and begin to create your own narrative. A narrative of peace. A story of love. A saga of contentment. It's called unleashing your creativity—something you have inside of you that's just waiting to emerge like a butterfly from its cocoon. Woman, you were born to create…because the Creator put the very best of His creativity into you. But you can only do that if you stop and lie back, allow your soul to awaken to its potential, and fearlessly discover your own unique power of expression.

AUGUST 12

I called on God and he answered.

JOB 12:4

Remember that time that you were in a crowded place—maybe a party you didn't want to go to, or one of those gatherings that you were coerced into attending. All you wanted to do was get out of there as quickly as possible, but the event seemed to go on interminably and you couldn't leave. So much of life can be like that. So, get comfortable with these situations. You can do it. You can't avoid every activity that takes you out of your comfort zone. In fact, aim to participate in them, because getting out of familiar waters is always an adventure worth having. Drift away from shore, every once in a while, and allow yourself to feel the freedom of not being in control of the situation. Let the waves come, and the waters churn. He will calm the storm. He's always watching, always vigilant, and always lovingly steering the boat.

AUGUST 13

⁓

I know that my redeemer lives,
and that in the end he will
stand on the earth.

JOB 19:25

Assurance is like armour. The armour that deflects the arrows of criticism and discouragement. It doesn't matter what the world thinks. You go out there and do your thing. Maybe you don't think you have the eloquence of one of your peers, but you have a strength that she doesn't. Discover what you're best at and capitalise on it. Use your strengths to advantage and build on your weaknesses. Don't let someone tell you that one side of your brain is more developed than the other. Your Heavenly Daddy gave you a full and complete brain and put all of its tremendous capabilities at your disposal. Give yourself time to discover all that you are capable of. Woman, your uniqueness is your defining power.

AUGUST 14

❧

I will see God; I myself will see him
with my own eyes—I, and not another.
How my heart yearns within me!

JOB 19:26-27

R un that marathon. Climb that mountain. Explore that woodland trail. You will see yourself as you never have before. You will discover facets to your character that you never knew existed. Woman, God lives in you, and as you grow into a deeper understanding of what this means, the more you will see Him in you. He is in the warm handshake or reassuring hug you give someone; the words you use to urge a fellow traveller to take another step forward on the trail, when reserves of energy are running low. He is in your heart as it swells with joy at the sounds of His creation— the rush of breeze or the gurgle of a stream. He is in your laughter when you throw your head back and look up at the sky, and feel exhilarated just to be alive and in this moment.

AUGUST 15

Submit to God and be at peace with him; in this way prosperity will come to you. Accept instruction from his mouth and lay up his words in your heart.

JOB 22:21-22

If your source of information and instruction is social media, you're going to be going around in circles because there's so much instruction and advice floating around in cyberspace. Imagine if you're following three different exercise regimens and four different diets, not to mention five different beauty plans because somehow that seemed to be the thing to do. Pretty soon you will find all of those diets and exercise routines warring against each other, and the results might not be what you expected. You are uniquely made. There is no 'one size fits all' health and beauty package. You need to follow what is specifically created to benefit you. Submit and surrender to your Creator God today and place yourself in His care. The peace that He places in your heart will give you a glow no beauty regimen can.

AUGUST 16

❧

*My feet have closely followed his steps; I
have kept to his way without turning aside.*

JOB 23:11

Ever walked in someone's footsteps? It's a fun thing to
do on the beach before the waves come and wash them
away. Or think of a trail that's been formed by constant use.
It's a safe route to follow and everyone can be assured of
getting to their destination by using it. Sometimes, it takes
stepping out of your comfort zone to follow a path created
by the Creator. You might be quite content to go your own
way, but He invites you every day to walk in the footsteps
that he has left for you…and they are never washed away,
never obliterated. There's a sense of comfort in following
them. You know that you have company. He's there with you.
And there are others following as well. It's a happy trail to
go on, because you know there are no dangers lurking along
the way. And even if there were any, He would take care of
them for you.

AUGUST 17

❧

I have not departed from the commands of his lips; I have treasured the words of his mouth more than my daily bread.

JOB 23:12

Today, call your mom and dad, and tell them that you love them. If you've been struggling in your relationship with them, then there's all the more reason to call them and just exchange news. Your mom will most likely ask if you've been eating right, sleeping enough, doing your laundry, and using that new detergent she told you about. Listen. Don't resent the questions, because they are prompted by love. Tell her that you hear her voice everytime you're tempted to skip breakfast, and that you remember the taste of that special dish she always cooked for you. One day, girl, you'll be a mom, and you'll be asking the same questions. Because the love of the Father dwells in your heart and this is how you show it. By being concerned. And by always hoping that the advice you gave is being followed.

AUGUST 18

༄

The Spirit of God has made me; the breath of the Almighty gives me life.

JOB 33:4

Chasing a fantasy may generally lead to a dead end. But following your dreams can lead you to a place of learning and transformation. Especially when you are following your dreams in the perfect Will of your Father God. That's why you need to remember that your life journey is different from everybody else's. The secret to your success lies in staying away from comparison. Focus on who you are and what you can, and need, to do. Don't follow somebody else's career path. You have your own. Your destiny is unique to you and you have been equipped with the talents and skills to achieve and accomplish your own unique goals. Today, think about where you are. Is this where you should be?

AUGUST 19

⁓

*God's voice thunders in marvelous ways; he
does great things beyond our understanding.*

JOB 37:5

You didn't think you could do it, but you did. You didn't
think you could ever get there, but you were able to.
Looking back, you will see how far you have come and
looking forward, may you be filled with anticipation of what
lies ahead. But right now, this moment, look at where your
feet are placed, and what direction you are facing in, and who
is in the room with you, and what sounds are clamouring
for your attention…and realise that even this moment has
its place of importance in the grand scheme of things. So,
try to find the treasure buried in the here and now. It might
be a clue to follow to the next phase, the next season. How
exciting life is—so fraught with adventure, and so filled with
promise…if you would but open your eyes and see!

AUGUST 20

I will give thanks to you, Lord, with all my heart; I will tell of all your wonderful deeds.

PSALM 9:1

It's so easy to wake up and complain—about the poor quality of sleep, the discomfort of the bed, the noise from outdoors that cut into your dreams...

Much harder to do is to be grateful even in the midst of the storm. Robert Brault says, '*Enjoy the little things, for one day you may look back and realise they were the big things.*' At night, if you find you can't sleep, maybe you were meant to wake up and listen to a sound from outside. Perhaps the song of a nightbird that will seal the moment and make it a precious memory. Or maybe you were meant to catch a glimpse of the moon sliding out from a blanket of cloud, to send a beam of warm light to wash over you. Perhaps you were meant to awaken to a new awareness of Him—your Creator, and to all of the wonders He created just for you. Say thank you, turn over and close your eyes. You will drift into blissful slumber.

AUGUST 21

❧

You are the helper of the fatherless.

PSALM 10:14

It's such a comfort to know that not only do we have our earthly dads, but we also have our Heavenly Father. He's the dad who watches over you constantly; protective of His baby girl, and always planning beautiful treats for her. He's with you when somebody treats you with kindness and He's with you when somone doesn't. When you're hurt, He steps between you and your attacker and shields you. He holds you close and comforts you. He is always there when you are on your own and don't have anyone else to reach out to. He will never let you down and he always has your back. Even your bestie may let you down, but your Best Daddy never will.

AUGUST 22

❧

*For in the gospel the righteousness of God
is revealed—a righteousness that is by
faith from first to last, just as it is written:
"The righteous will live by faith."*

ROMANS 1:17

Martin Luther King Jr. said, "Faith is taking the first step, even when you don't see the whole staircase." It is going down a dark alleyway because you can see a sliver of light in the distance. Faith is knowing that no matter what, your future is taken care of—secure—because God spoke over it and ordained it to be so. It is waking up and going through your day without needless anxiety over what may be or what could be. Cast aside all uncertainty and doubt, because it only detracts from your peace and keeps you away from God's plan. Follow His voice to your destination. Follow it with the faith of a courageous woman.

AUGUST 23

To those who by persistence in doing good seek glory, honor and immortality, he will give eternal life.

ROMANS 2:7

Someday when you go on a road trip, perhaps like a rite of passage, to mark a transition from one phase of life to another, focus on the emotions that assail you as you travel. The road, like the sea or the sky, is suspended in between two points—the one you left and the one you are moving towards. While you drive you have the facility, or distraction, of a rear-view mirror, to warn you of what's behind. In life, which is another kind of journey, don't let the images in the rear-view mirror of your mind, rob you of the joy of the ride and the bliss of looking ahead.

AUGUST 24

⁓

And all are justified freely by his grace through the redemption that came by Christ Jesus.

ROMANS 3:24

Getting out of a painful situation—or relationship—is like being redeemed. It's like having the chains snapped from your wrists and your life bought back for you, to have a second chance at living it the way you were meant to. It's something to ponder on. Think of a prisoner who has been pardoned and released. He would probably live each day like it was his last…because he has known the fear of never being able to see the light of freedom again. Today, think of yourself—a trapped butterfly, suddenly finding an escape route…or being gently assisted out into the bright light of a new day. It's time to throw your hands into the air and twirl away, celebrating your freedom.

AUGUST 25

~

Therefore, since we have been justified through faith, we have peace with God through our Lord Jesus Christ.

ROMANS 5:1

Barbara Johnson said, *'Faith is seeing light with your heart, when all your eyes see is darkness.'* That light that your heart perceives, reassures you that you can go forward with confidence; that the darkness will have to yield to the light very soon. Trying situations come and go. They determine your staying power and your ability to see past the storm to the rainbow. Today, wake up with hope in your heart and with gratitude for getting another chance at getting life right. Rest easy. Sleep sound. Be of good cheer. You cleared the first few hurdles. You can get past the rest.

AUGUST 26

⤳

We have gained access by faith into
this grace in which we now stand. And
we boast in the hope of the glory of God.

Imagine the most exclusive group in school. The clique you observe from afar and wistfully imagine that you will belong to one day. Well, you belong to the most exclusive group ever, and you haven't gained access to it by being a certain way, or having certain things. You were just invited because The Lord of Heaven's Armies decided you were to have access to it, simply because of His grace. What will you do with your new-found status? How will you treat yourself, and how will you relate to the rest of the world from this unique standpoint? How you operate is determined by your strength and courage. So, woman, stand strong and true.

AUGUST 27

❧

Not only so, but we also glory in our
sufferings, because we know that suffering
produces perseverance; perseverance,
character; and character, hope.

ROMANS 5:3-4

Have you been on a trek lately? If you haven't, maybe it's time to plan one. Be adventurous. Go off the oft-used trail. Take the path less travelled. Enjoy your solitude as you walk along. Connect with your innermost thoughts and revel in the beauty you have the privilege to enjoy. The miles will fly by and save you from feeling so weary that you wonder if you can go on. Stick with the path and make a sincere effort not to quit because you're not sure if you should even be doing this. You were meant to conquer the trail. You were made to own your life. Woman, keep at it. You will get there because you were made to.

AUGUST 28

❧

But I trust in your unfailing love;
my heart rejoices in your salvation.

PSALM 13:5

Unbreakable. Unshakeable. That's who you are. Tenacious. Vivacious. That's who you are. Unstoppable. Unforgettable. That's who you are. Your beauty has been sung of. You're one of a kind. Yet modest, and humble, you know your mind. Sweet teacher of children, pathbreaker, earth shaker, you are who you are because that's how you were made. Larger than life, you make a statement wherever you go. Because Woman, you own the show. Oh, how you've grown, how you've progressed, how much you have learned. Through the darkness and rough weather, you came, broken but not beaten, made whole by His love. Oh Woman, dear woman, gentle as a dove, yet strong as a Lion with strength from above.

AUGUST 29

*I will sing the Lord's praise,
for he has been good to me.*

PSALM 13:6

When the rain comes down, dance in the downpour. Life is all about making the most of every situation and finding the good in the midst of something that's not great. When you walk through the storm, invite someone to share your umbrella and make a new friend. When the flood waters rise, don't be afraid, Jesus will walk across the waves and rescue you. Remember that courage is stubborn faith. Your tenacity is your signature. So, hold on and don't let go. There's no room for apprehension where courage rules. Chase the storm away with a song and create an atmosphere of healing wherever you go.

AUGUST 30

⌁

Lord, you alone are my portion and my cup;
you make my lot secure.

PSALM 16:5

I n a world where the threats to a woman's safety seem to only escalate, it's a comfort to know that faith in God's protection alleviates the anxiety of navigating this life on your own. Always remember that while you may be vulnerable, you are not weak. It doesn't even take karate classes to prove you are strong and able to hold your own. Woman, you're a fighter, an overcomer, because you have God on your side. You are tenacious. You don't give up easily. Keep honing those strengths. The more you use them, the sharper they become. Today, focus on your strength—that power that comes from deep inside of you, because you have the Spirit of God within you. Draw on it. Use it. Take refuge in it. It keeps you safe and secure.

AUGUST 31

❧

I will praise the Lord, who counsels me;
even at night my heart instructs me.

PSALM 16:7

Waking from a nightmare can be unsettling. Most nightmares are realistic, and it takes a while to shake off the terror that accompanies one of these bad dreams. The next time you wake from a nightmare, begin to praise your Heavenly Father. Take time to talk to Him. Seek His counsel. Pour out your heart to Him. He dispels the terrors of a nightmare in a single breath. Discovering, and reaching into, the power of prayer is crucial. Keep the dialogue with your Father God alive. Yes, it's not a monologue, but a two-way conversation. You ask and He answers. At night, when the world is still, it's even easier to hear His voice.

NOTES

_____

_____

_____

_____

_____

_____

_____

_____

_____

_____

_____

_____

SEPTEMBER

SEPTEMBER 1

❧

*Your throne, O God, will last for
ever and ever; a scepter of justice will
be the scepter of your kingdom.*

HEBREWS 1:8

There will always be signs of injustice in the world. Maybe you were once the target of prejudice and discrimination. You can do something about it. As a woman of strength and faith, you can do your bit towards alleviating the bitter results of unfairness and intolerance. Your spontaneous empathy could heal a broken heart. Your innate desire to nurture and nourish the downtrodden could turn things around in many lives. God has a special plan for you, dear woman. You were created with His heart, and you have His vision to see justice done. So, take up your weapons of kindness, goodness and gentleness, and fight this war with His hand of protection and guidance upon you.

SEPTEMBER 2

~⌒~

Therefore God, your God, has set you above your companions by anointing you with the oil of joy.

HEBREWS 1:9

Laughter, they say, is the best medicine. So, if you're feeling under the weather, depressed or discouraged, tune into something that will make you laugh. Take a stroll on a country road, if you can, or drive out to a farm. Watch sheep gambolling and lambs play. Watch kittens frolic and ducks teach their young ones how to swim. Or get together with a friend and recall those fun times when you were little, and up to mischief. Joy is your birthright. Happiness is your natural state of being. To be downcast is to go against your very nature. Today, may your cup of joy overflow and impact those around you.

SEPTEMBER 3

~

We must pay the most careful attention,
therefore, to what we have heard,
so that we do not drift away.

HEBREWS 2:1

When you know what's good and true, hold fast to it. Don't allow it to be replaced by wrong advice, or opinions that don't match what you know to be right. Don't let wisecracks steal your wisdom. Stand for what you believe in, because you were created to effect change where it is needed. The world is filled with noise and chatter. Wherever you go, you are assailed by the voices of unbelief and cynicism. But you glow with an inner light. You have the power of His presence. You pave the way for others to follow. Go forward with confidence and courage. You have reserves of strength that you haven't tapped into yet!

SEPTEMBER 4

❧

Because he himself suffered when
he was tempted, he is able to help
those who are being tempted.

HEBREWS 2:18

Even the strongest person is subject to temptation, but you needn't become a subject of temptation, or a victim. Get on its head and stomp it down. Flatten it. You can. What is it, after all, but hollow allure, which you can see through. You know when it's coming at you. You have an innate ability to discern the signs. It seems innocent at first, like a cloud of cotton candy—beckoning to you to enjoy something that you know will only lead to certain destruction. Confront it head on, secure in the knowledge that He who overcame temptation is by your side to give you victory over it.

SEPTEMBER 5

❧

*But Christ is faithful as the Son over
God's house. And we are his house, if
indeed we hold firmly to our confidence
and the hope in which we glory.*

HEBREWS 3:6

Hope is our natural inclination to look forward in anticipation of better things to come. Hope is a gift from God, wrapped in a covering of faith. Franklin D. Roosevelt said, '*We have always held to the hope, the belief, the conviction that there is a better life, a better world, beyond the horizon.*' It's always there, in the back of our minds, that something will change for the better when we turn the next corner. Don't wait till the next corner to entertain Hope. Be a good host to it. Let Hope remain in your house, because as long as it remains, you will keep believing that the closed doors will swing open; the windows of opportunity will part at your touch, and that a new sun will rise on a rosy horizon. And when you believe, and continue to hope…things do happen!

SEPTEMBER 6

～

But encourage one another daily, as
long as it is called "Today".

HEBREWS 3:13

Today is significant. Today is the *present* and therefore a gift from God. Why spend this gift of the present either ruing the past or lamenting the future? Why not use it in the best way possible, by valuing it? So, here's a thought. You woke up this morning. Which basically means that you were meant to. If you were meant to, that means that there was something specific that God wanted you to accomplish, receive or do, today, that would be for your wellbeing or the wellbeing of someone else. Today, try to discover what this might be. It might just be because you were meant to give somebody a word of advice or encouragement. Or it might be because you were meant to pay someone a visit that would prevent them from feeling that they were unwanted or unloved. Discover the significance of this day, this hour, this moment, and in so doing, discover your own significance on this planet.

SEPTEMBER 7

⁓

There remains, then, a Sabbath-rest for the people of God; for anyone who enters God's rest also rests from their works, just as God did from his. Let us, therefore, make every effort to enter that rest, so that no one will perish by following their example of disobedience.

HEBREWS 4:9-11

Beautiful girl, you need your rest. You don't need to work 24x7. Whoever made you believe that, isn't doing you any favours. Keep your sanity and your beauty by allowing your system a day to wind down and be at peace. It's important. Not to follow this simple, yet vital, rule, is to invite trouble. Tiredness invites sickness, and if your body isn't in a fit state to fight off all those ever present germs in the atmosphere, you will be losing more days being sick than if you were to take a day off work every week. Your day of rest is also a day to reconnect with yourself and your loved ones. Honour this time.

SEPTEMBER 8

❦

*Therefore, since we have a great
high priest who has ascended into
heaven, Jesus the Son of God, let us
hold firmly to the faith we profess.*

HEBREWS 4:14

It's so great to have someone who's on your side. Someone who is interceding with your Heavenly daddy to make things better for you. So, while the world is losing hold of what's important, you hold on. Because you know, first hand, how important you are to God, and how much He loves you. Give somebody hope today. Tell them how their lives can change too, and how they don't need to be anxious… because all their needs are being met even as they are thinking of them.

SEPTEMBER 9

❧

Let us then approach God's throne
of grace with confidence, so that we
may receive mercy and find grace
to help us in our time of need.

HEBREWS 4:16

Do you know what's so amazing about this faith? It is that no matter what you have done in the past, your father God isn't ever going to deny you what you ask for—because He is only concerned with the present. So, the awesome thing is, you don't need to feel like you're too unworthy to receive things you request, because you failed to measure up to His standards. The world has all these standards, but your Heavenly Daddy doesn't. He just wants you to come to Him as you are, and He lovingly transforms you into who you were made to be. What's more, He's always there to help you whenever you need.

SEPTEMBER 10

༒

But solid food is for the mature, who
by constant use have trained themselves
to distinguish good from evil.

Hebrews 5:14

Remember how you used to talk 'baby talk' as a…well…
as a *baby*? And how your parents also communicated
with you with this same baby talk? Well girl, now you're
all grown up, so if your mom or dad tell it like it is, just
remember, you're ready for *solid food*. Solid food helps you
grow and mature. This is the time for 'grown-up' stuff, like
having a mature conversation… and being mature enough
to handle good, constructive criticism which is meant to
help you grow. Beautiful woman, you are meant for bigger
things, so don't get all petty about something that somebody
said which you didn't like. Sure, it hurt. But that's probably
because it touched a raw nerve. Get up and get on with it.
There's no time or place for self-pity. You are better than that!

SEPTEMBER 11

❧

Land that drinks in the rain often falling on It, and that produces a crop useful to those for whom it is farmed, receives the blessing of God.

HEBREWS 6:7

People tell you things for your good. Mentors will instruct you. How much are you drinking in and retaining? Are you allowing good advice to sink deep, like a seed going into the soil, and are you watering it with your acceptance and encouraging it to sprout and grow? Or are you witholding the warmth and the water, so that the seed cannot ever become a plant, with the promise of a blessed harvest? Think about this today. How well do you use opportunities to learn and grow? How well do you use criticism as a springboard to help you improve and set better personal goals? Is failure to accept helpful advice from others stunting your growth?

SEPTEMBER 12

~

I will put my laws in their minds and write them on their hearts. I will be their God, and they will be my people.

HEBREWS 8:10

Isn't it great to walk with the confidence that comes from knowing that you know the truth and that it is imprinted on your heart? The truth is simply this, you are loved, and you were made to love others. You were made to be joyful and to flourish. You were made to be successful and to overcome challenges. If the world came against you, you would be victorious over it. Because you were made to be victorious. Why is this so? Because you are a Daughter of the Most High God; the Creator of the universe who loves you more than you can even begin to comprehend. He equips you and keeps pouring His strength into you every time you need to be refreshed. So, girl, go out there and shine like the star that you are!

SEPTEMBER 13

᳗

So Christ was sacrificed once to take away the sins of many; and he will appear a second time, not to bear sin, but to bring salvation to those who are waiting for him.

HEBREWS 9:28

The verb to wait sounds terious, doesn't it? In January, waiting for Christmas can seem like a long wait, but come November, and suddenly you're feeling 'unprepared'. You need to get things done in time. You need to go shopping and buy gifts. There are endless lists to deal with. Suddenly Christmas is upon you. The hour has come. Wouldn't it be ideal if, while waiting, you were getting all your shopping done, a few gifts per month, maybe, and enjoying the whole process of waiting? Well, this doesn't only pertain to Christmas but to waiting in general. While you wait for your big break, savour the small achievements. It will make the wait seem less interminable and definitely worthwhile.

SEPTEMBER 14

Let us draw near to God with a sincere heart and with the full assurance that faith brings, having our hearts sprinkled to cleanse us from a guilty conscience and having our bodies washed with pure water.

HEBREWS 10:22

Cleansing is an important ritual for every woman. You need to get that layer of make-up off so that your pores don't get clogged. You need to assiduously work the cleanser over every inch of your facial skin to ensure its ultimate health. Wouldn't it be great if your skin automatically cleansed itself? Or if it had a built-in mechanism that would render it cleansed even if you still had your makeup on? Thank God for His amazing gift that has cleansed your soul once and for all, so that you never have to entertain guilt or shame no matter what your past has been like. You have a permanent 'cleanser' that has worked within you. So draw near to Him with faith and assurance that He, your Heavenly Daddy, will regard you with love and favour when you approach Him with your concerns and requests.

SEPTEMBER 15

~e

Let us hold unswervingly to the hope we profess, for he who promised is faithful.

HEBREWS 10:23

Remember the time when you asked a parent for something and they couldn't, or didn't, or failed to, meet your need or request? Maybe there was a valid reason for it, or maybe there wasn't any reason except a failure to remember a promise that was made. Loved ones are fallible, like all of humanity. Only God is perfect and good, always coming through on His promises. Faith is the ability to hold on, despite a long wait, in the expectation of the promise being fulfilled. But there is only one person we can repose such unquestioning faith in, and that is God. Human beings will invariably let you down. Forgive the transgression. You may have let someone down too and you were forgiven. It's best to understand human weakness and to accept it... holding on instead, and trusting in, the infallible strength of Him who calls you *His Child*.

SEPTEMBER 16

༄

And let us consider how we may spur one another on toward love and good deeds.

HEBREWS 10:24

Imagine a field of flowers or a vineyard filled with ripe grapes. Imagine a large team of harvesters—picking the flowers and harvesting the grapes. They laugh and talk as they work. Maybe they sing together. Imagine if the whole world worked in unison that way—sowing, reaping and sharing. What a beautiful thing would be this oneness that drew people together in a circle of love and goodwill. How blessed we all would be. Today, get together with your friends on a simple project. Perhaps make something beautiful together. Share your skills. You could pool your resources to make an embroidered quilt or a bunch of Christmas Cards. There's pleasure in the pursuit of simple activities that bring people together in an atmosphere of love and sharing. The heavens see it and smile.

SEPTEMBER 17

❧

*So do not throw away your confidence; it
will be richly rewarded.*

HEBREWS 10:35

If you haven't been feeling quite so brave lately, or quite so gung-ho about something you were super charged about—probably because somebody, or something, burst your bubble…cheer up, because we've all been there. The thing about confidence, is that it comes and goes—if you allow it to be that dependant on what people say, or on prevailing circumstances. Remaining confident is reliant only on one thing—your faith in God and His ability to do all the heavy lifting when you can't. You can do all things— because He is with you. You are not alone in this. He is working in and through you. Stray strong girl. Don't lose your focus. Look at who's inside of you, instead of what's in front of you.

SEPTEMBER 18

❧

You need to persevere so that when you have done the will of God, you will receive what he has promised.

HEBREWS 10:36

What counts is that you finish the marathon, and not whether you come in first. Follow through with what you begin—finish that collage you were making, or the sweater you were knitting; complete the scrapbook of memories or the painting you began. It matters little how long you take. What counts is that you stay the course and finish. Life is a marathon. Keeping your faith burning bright is what gets you through it, and also what enables you to help others along the way. Be the runner who picks up someone who has fallen by the wayside and gives him a drink of water, a word of encouragement, and a helping hand to get going again.

SEPTEMBER 19

~

*But we do not belong to those who
shrink back and are destroyed, but to
those who have faith and are saved.*

HEBREWS 10:39

Today, don't begin to discuss your problems, but instead ask somebody how they are feeling. As you empathise with what someone else is going through, and as you point them to a life lived in faith, your own faith is strengthened. You grow by helping others live life more fully. You weren't meant to dwell in isolation. This life is not just for you. It is meant to be shared. Every once in a while, invite someone to have a meal with you that you have prepared. It might not be a gourmet feast, but pour a lot of love and care into it. With each meal you will make a friend, and maybe even save a soul in distress.

SEPTEMBER 20

&

Now faith is confidence in what we hope
for and assurance about what we do not see.

HEBREWS 11:1

A friend told you about the most incredible food she had ever had. It was in a restaurant quite a distance away, but you feel encouraged to find your way there, because your friend said that the food was too good to miss. You go by what your friend says. You see her eyes shine as she describes the meal, course by course. You feel the excitement of partaking of a spread as divine as she describes it to be. You have faith that she would never encourage you to drive miles away for something that would disappoint you. Think about your faith today—in things not seen, and never to be experienced in this world. Things that you get a whisper of or taste in part—the things that your Father God reveals. How firm is your faith? How far are you willing to go, to experience the feast He has assured you will be every bit worth the wait and the long journey?

SEPTEMBER 21

❧

*God had planned something better
for us so that only together with us
would they be made perfect.*

HEBREWS 11:40

Remember when you were little, and you had a dolls' tea party or attended one that your friend invited you to? Maybe you made pizza out of play dough and cookies out of clay. You pretended to eat, and you made believe that the dolls relished every bit of this feast. At the end of it your mom came in and laid out a tea that was edible, and it was delicious. She didn't do it on a whim. She had planned it all along because she knew you kids would be hungry for real food at some point. Your Heavenly Father is like that. You might have plans, but He has something better and bigger lined up for you. Something more substantial. What joy you will feel when you discover what it is!

SEPTEMBER 22

Therefore, since we are surrounded by such a great cloud of witnesses, let us throw off everything that hinders and the sin that so easily entangles. And let us run with perseverance the race marked out for us.

HEBREWS 12:1

Try running a race with your legs tied—not simple, right? No matter how badly you want to reach the finish line, you will keep falling over and hurting yourself. In all probability, you will give up because the task seems impossible. Being weighed down by excess baggage—memories, hurt, anger, disappointment—is like that. They are the chains that bind you and keep you from making progress. It's important to remind yourself every day that you don't need to carry all of this around. Lay it aside, because it was taken care of when Jesus died for you. Move forward without the weight of your past holding you back. You'll soon see what a difference it makes to your progress.

SEPTEMBER 23

～

Do not make light of the Lord's discipline,
and do not lose heart when he rebukes you,
because the Lord disciplines the one he loves,
and he chastens everyone he accepts as his...

HEBREWS 12:5-6

When you wake up, heaven smiles and sends a ray of sunlight down just for you—to warm you up and make you smile. A little bird hops onto your window-sill and cheeps hopefully for a crumb, making you chuckle. You feel happy and loved. Because you were made to be happy and loved. You are a child of God, so step into the joy of having the Creator look out for you every minute of each day. But when you choose to take a path that He never intended for you to take, maybe, for a while, the world may go a little dark. But His eye is still upon you. He calls out. Maybe you don't hear because you are so intent upon discovering this new path. But when you call out to Him, He hears. He always hears. Because he's always listening. And soon He leads you back to safety—and you're warm and free once again. Maybe, next time around, stay with the path He set out for you. It's the only one worth travelling along.

SEPTEMBER 24

Endure hardship as discipline; God is treating you as his children. For what children are not disciplined by their father?

Exams are tough, aren't they? They're meant to be. They are a systematic assessment of what you have learned. Life has its tests and exams too. They shape, mould and form you. In a crisis you learn how to use whatever resources are available to you. You learn how to deal with different challenges. Above all, you learn how to rely on a Provider who is bigger than you and all of this earth. At the other side of every test and struggle is a reward. A prize for holding on and not letting go. It's a gift of love. An assurance from your Heavenly Father, that He is with you no matter what. The night may seem long, but dawn is just around the corner.

SEPTEMBER 25

❧

No discipline seems pleasant at the time,
but painful. Later on, however, it produces
a harvest of righteousness and peace for
those who have been trained by it.

HEBREWS 12:11

A sportsperson will tell you how gruelling the training is. To get in shape to win against a powerful adversary, takes long hours of stamina building exercises and practice to perfect their technique. This season may seem difficult—with hurdles to surmount at every turn. You're growing weary of it all, and you wonder if there will be an end to it. Cheer up, because every weight you carry is building your character. Every hurdle you clear is making you sharper, and more focused. Every trial you undergo is refining and perfecting you. You are getting stronger girl. And the bonus is that you will have a story to tell everyone around you—of how you prevailed, despite the odds, and emerged a winner! With His help of course!

SEPTEMBER 26

❧

Make every effort to live in peace
with everyone and to be holy; without
holiness no one will see the Lord.

HEBREWS 12:14

Wouldn't it be a perfect world without any wars? Wouldn't it be great to have no conflict at all? But how do you achieve such a state of peace and tranquility? First find peace within yourself. If you can do that, you would win half the battle. People, most often, become tranquil around peaceful people. When the atmosphere is calm, there seems to be no need to disturb it. Peace is especially accessible when everyone is being built up—equally. Share your resources. Be happy to teach someone else what you have learned. Competition is good, but never at the cost of peace. On your way to the top, how many will you take along with you?

SEPTEMBER 27

❧

Therefore, since we are receiving a kingdom that cannot be shaken, let us be thankful, and so worship God acceptably with reverence and awe.

HEBREWS 12:28

How many times have you been to the beach and gazed out across the horizon and thought, not about the sea itself, but about that great and powerful force that separated water from land and contained the water so that it served its purpose without wreaking constant havoc? How many times have you watched the sun set—seeming as if it's sinking into the waves in the distance; throwing its striking light across the water—and wondered at this life-giving force of energy that is way up in the sky and yet feels so close? Have you stood there and felt the breath of God in the wind and realised how, unlike the sun, He moves, even in the very air around you, and is close…so very close? How many times have you said, as you enjoy the spectacular world He created, *'From the bottom of my heart, Oh Lord, I thank you'*?

SEPTEMBER 28

Keep on loving one another as brothers and sisters. Do not forget to show hospitality to strangers, for by so doing some people have shown hospitality to angels without knowing it.

HEBREWS 13:1-2

Dear wonderful woman, you are so special. In fact, you are so special that there are people who want to know you better. They want to hear your story. They want to know how you do the things you do. They are curious about what makes you tick. If you've become accustomed to keeping to yourself, because it's comfortable, then today, think about reaching out to someone who looks like they could use a friend. There are lots of people like that, whose smiles conceal the world of pain they are actually in. You could be the salve to their wounds. So, you're not the world's best cook, but maybe you could call your mom for a recipe—or look one up online. But have somebody over. It will help you discover more about yourself even as you discover more about someone else.

SEPTEMBER 29

~

Keep your lives free from the love of money and be content with what you have, because God has said, "Never will I leave you; never will I forsake you."

HEBREWS 13:5

It's important to have money to meet your needs. It's equally important that money not become all important. Recall those happy days when a full piggy bank meant you could buy the world. You lived your life secure in the knowledge that you were provided for, and you never really gave it much thought. But suddenly, money has assumed a position of great significance and is not just a piggy bank on your bedside table. In the pursuit of it, you are risking friendships, family and your health. Take a step back and reassess your life. What are you placing at the center? What ought to be at the center? It's not to late to make a change that will transform your life. Remember that your Father God is a loving parent who provides well for His children.

SEPTEMBER 30

❧

*So we say with confidence, "The Lord
is my helper; I will not be afraid.
What can mere mortals do to me?"*

HEBREWS 13:6

So, you're travelling in a strange country or navigating unfamiliar territory at school or your workplace. You feel your confidence ebb when you should be feeling on top of your game. No matter what you do, you feel intimidated, and you just wish you could pluck up enough courage to just relax and feel at home. Don't be anxious. You will soon get the hang of things. It takes a little trial and error to find your way around the problem, but you will get there. Just have faith—in God and in yourself too. Remind yourself that you can't lose when you have the King of Kings on your side. Go on—make that speech, stand for that election, make that trip, visit that person…

If you don't do it now you will be missing out on the experience of a lifetime. Don't let fear rob you of your fun.

NOTES

_____

_____

_____

_____

_____

_____

_____

_____

_____

_____

_____

OCTOBER

OCTOBER 1

*And do not forget to do good and
to share with others, for with such
sacrifices God is pleased.*

HEBREWS 13:16

Woman, you are so blessed. You have the favour of God upon you. You have been created to accomplish great things. You have also been given a rare and wonderful gift—a caring, empathetic spirit and a giving heart. Give and it will be given to you. You will discover how sharing doubles your joy. Reach out to someone who is lonely or discouraged and you will feel more fulfilled than you ever have before. You don't need to be a millionnaire to help somebody in need. Share your last dollar and God will fill up your purse because of your acts of kindness. And if you don't have anything to give, give someone a smile or a hug…and you will receive abundant joy in return!

OCTOBER 2

⁓

*Have confidence in your leaders and submit
to their authority, because they keep watch
over you as those who must give an account.*

Hebrews 13:17

I t's sometimes difficult to bow, so to speak, to those placed in leadership positions above you. You might feel resentful of the fact that you have to capitulate to them when you don't feel inclined to do so. It could be your parents, or teachers and instructors in school. Your greatness lies in your humility, and your ability to acknowledge that you owe them your respect and obedience. One day you will be in a position of authority and may face the prospect that the team you lead might not always be ready and willing to see your point of view. But when you do the right thing and give respect now, then it comes back to you when it's your turn to receive it.

OCTOBER 3

~

Now may the God of peace... equip you with everything good for doing his will, and may he work in us what is pleasing to him...

Think about a well—that source of water that in times gone by used to be the center of every community. If you dug a well, a town would spring up around it. Because a well gives—yielding up all that it has, of pure, life-giving water. The thing about being a woman is that you are, by nature, that life-giving source. You have a natural born ability to love unconditionally and to give till it hurts. Your hands open to those in need and you know what to say when somebody needs to hear a few words of comfort. You are like a well, around which a whole community gathers. As you grow in your role, you will realise the increasing sphere of your influence. What's truly remarkable is how you will automatically evolve, and be equipped, by the very hand of your Maker. Don't be afraid to step into your role right now, no matter how young you think you are, because you are more ready than you know!

OCTOBER 4

❧

*I call on you, my God, for you
will answer me; turn your ear to
me and hear my prayer. Show me
the wonders of your great love.*

PSALM 17:6-7

Road trips are such fun. Just about anything can happen on one. For instance, you could stop somewhere and meet somebody you might never have met if you hadn't taken that trip or stopped at precisely that moment. Think of this season of your life as a road trip. You're driving along—perhaps with a road map, or maybe you've decided to go where the trail leads. Often, along the way, you stop for a rest, or to eat. Who do you meet and what do you talk about? Today, stop for a while and talk to your Heavenly Daddy. He hasn't heard from you in a while and He really wants a chance to tell you how much He loves you and cares about you. He might also want to tell you that the trail you're on might not be the safest or the best and that you might want to take a different route. Make time on this journey to stop and listen to Him. He's always got something important to say, personally, to you!

OCTOBER 5

The Lord is my rock, my fortress and my deliverer; my God is my rock, in whom I take refuge, my shield and the horn of my salvation, my stronghold.

PSALM 18:2

Whenever you're feeling particularly vulnerable or unsafe, let your imagination transport you to the crest of a mountain or the ramparts of a castle. There you can lie, safe in the knowledge that nothing can prevail against you. This mountain and these ramparts are strong and impenetrable, and nothing can get past them. They are created by the very love of The Lord, who protects and defends His little girl. He will never let the terrors of the night or the threats of the day come against you. He has placed you on earth for a specific purpose, and He holds you close and safe, because He won't let anything get in the way of His Will for your life. So, chin up, girl, you've got Heaven's armies fighting for you!

OCTOBER 6

❧

He reached down from on high and took
hold of me; he drew me out of deep waters.
He rescued me from my powerful enemy,
from my foes, who were too strong for me.

PSALM 18:16-17

It's a beautiful feeling to dance in the rain. The cooling showers on your face, and in your hair, release you from the shackles that have prevented you from letting go until now. For a while you let your guard down, and allow yourself to be swept away by the downpour. There's such a sense of freedom; of escaping from all your cares. Nothing seems to matter but that you're alive and revelling in that moment. It's the same way you feel when you surrender all your burdens to The Lord and just allow yourself to experience the joy of being free in His love. It's funny to think about, but here's what it is—the more you hand over to Him, the stronger and more in control you are. To truly be successful in life, and at peace with yourself and the world, hold your hands up to him and let Him lift you out of your situation and take over.

OCTOBER 7

As for God, his way is perfect:
The Lord's word is flawless; he
shields all who take refuge in him.

PSALM 18:30

People say so many things all the time. Words are often misused. You might be carrying some hurt linked to a memory or memories of things people said to you. Words do break you, contrary to what people say or think. Words are powerful tools of influence. Words can heal, build-up or destroy. Today, let go of the memories or hurt you have felt over words that you were assaulted with. Carrying them around can only cause long term damage and hold you back from the bright future God has created for you to step into. While you let go of your memories, also ask for forgiveness in case your words have caused hurt to someone else. And after you do that, speak a positive word into someone's life. It might be the one bright thing that happened to them today.

OCTOBER 8

～

*It is God who arms me with strength
and keeps my way secure. He makes
my feet like the feet of a deer; he
causes me to stand on the heights.*

PSALM 18:32-33

Have you ever watched a deer run? It's legs barely seem to touch the ground. Its movements are so fluid, effortless. It doesn't think about how it's going to move. It just relies on its ability to do so. When a predator is stalking it, it flees with such speed, yet remains ever graceful. Today, beautiful woman, walk with greater confidence, covered by the Grace of your Protector. You were made to win. You were designed to conquer. Stay confident in your abilities and talents. Know that nothing can get in the way of your progress forward. Be someone's inspiration. Motivate someone with your self-belief, and the assurance that you draw from the love of your Heavenly Father.

OCTOBER 9

❦

He trains my hands for battle; my
arms can bend a bow of bronze.

PSALM 18:34

G irl, you are stronger than you think. Okay, so you've been crying a lot lately. You don't feel like you can take another setback. But think of a bow and arrow. The bow has to be drawn back for the arrow to be propelled forward. There's something big ahead for you. Don't give up. Just hang in there. The best is yet to come. The setback will lead to the big push forward. So, keep setting those goals and dreaming your dreams. Keep buoyed up with a positive attitude. You'll get there. In the meantime, get the best out of the situation. Take time to introspect and seek the will of the Lord. Enjoy the company of your friends and loved ones. Discover something new that you can learn from them, and something new that you can share with them. You're young. The doors you're knocking at will open soon.

OCTOBER 10

You make your saving help my shield,
and your right hand sustains me;
your help has made me great.

PSALM 18:35

When you're caught in a storm and seek shelter, you choose the kind that's dependable and won't let the rain in; a place of refuge where you aren't exposed to the onslaught. In life, friends are the refuge that you seek when you are in the midst of rough weather. Choose the most reliable and trustworthy; the kind that will not let you down or sell you out. Friendships are like lifeboats—helping you escape from the rigours of life's storms. Give yourself completely to them. Don't hold back and shut yourself in. Be the friend that others seek to know and turn to in a crisis. Be the strong shoulder that somebody can cry on. Be the helping hand reaching out through the bleak mists of hopelessness. Remember, you were created in God's image, and He is always the best friend to have. Today, assess your friendships, and evaluate, honestly, if you've been a good friend to others.

OCTOBER 11

༄

The law of the Lord is perfect, refreshing the soul. The statutes of the Lord are trustworthy, making wise the simple.

PSALM 19:7

There is one rule that you should keep—to live life to its fullest. No matter how crammed your schedule is; no matter how many commitments you have to keep, always make time to seek the will of God for your life. So much of what you can do with your life and your time gets obliterated by a sea of commitments, and you forget that you actually have to live rather than merely exist. Today, look for a stray bloom rising up through the cracks in the sidewalk, and in so doing discover the poet inside of you; or just look within yourself and study the many facets of your personality. Perhaps you never knew that you would make a fine teacher because of your patience and desire to share knowledge. Maybe you never considered your artistic side, or the fact that you are actually quite scientifically minded. One thing about heaven's rules is that they are never restrictive and are always in place to give you the freedom to discover who you really are.

OCTOBER 12

〜

*The precepts of the Lord are
right, giving joy to the heart.
The commands of the Lord are
radiant, giving light to the eyes.*

PSALM 19:8

It's time to get your eyesight checked. Or should we say *'I' sight*? Have you ever thought about the term '*myopia*'? Well, the dictionary gives it two meanings—to be *short sighted*, and *lack of foresight or intellectual insight.* There is a third way to look at the word—'*my*''opia' (opia being a visual disorder). Okay, so you probably have guessed where this is going. Today, think about what your personal *visual disorder* is. How do you perceive things? How do you look at the life that you have been given? How do you feel about your role in your school, college, family or community? What do you think you could, or should do, in order to transform your outlook? Do you think you need to put on a pair of *rose-tinted glasses* every once in a while, to remind yourself just how good you've got it, and how much better you could make it for someone else who needs your help?

OCTOBER 13

❧

The fear of the Lord is pure,
enduring forever. The decrees
of the Lord are firm, and all
of them are righteous.

PSALM 19:9

What do you do when someone tells you to follow a specific code of conduct and you think your way is better, or the only way? Some might think it's a good idea to get different points of view and then use them like ingredients in a dish—basically mesh them all together and see how things turn out. You will, perhaps, find that the dish you've created has conflicting flavours and nothing seems to blend harmoniously together. The ingredients haven't been created to be used simultaneously in one dish. The result is confusion. It's good to know, at this point, that with Jesus there is just one law to follow. Love. Love God. Love people. Even love your enemies. When you do that, you will never want to hurt, betray, or do anything other than elevate and be good to the ones you love. Without exception or barriers. He created a perfect law and in keeping it, you are set free in a way you never imagined.

OCTOBER 14

～

Now this I know: The Lord gives victory to his anointed. He answers him from his heavenly sanctuary with the victorious power of his right hand.

PSALM 20:6

Have you ever been lonely and just needed to talk to somebody, and after much hesitation you dialled the number of a friend you thought might care? Did you hold your breath while the phone kept ringing almost plaintively? Did you wish you hadn't called? Did you feel 'exposed', humiliated and mortified when the person didn't answer? Did you send them a text message a few minutes later saying, *'Oops, I might have dialled your number by mistake,'*? Did you follow that with an emojee expressing some emotion that was diametrically opposite to everything you were feeling? Next time you need someone to talk to, or a strong shoulder to lean on, just say a prayer. It's a spiritual phone call to your Heavenly Daddy and He always responds!

OCTOBER 15

❧

Some trust in chariots and some in horses, but we trust in the name of the Lord our God.

PSALM 20:7

"How fast can you get here?" somebody asks. "*Time's running out.*" Yes, there's almost always a sense of urgency about everything. It's like you're living under a constant threat of dire consequences if you don't get somewhere very *fast.* Life has become so rushed that it seems like quite often you are running somewhere and you don't even know why you're in such a self-imposed hurry. You're either rushing or chasing something down, or playing catch-up. The sense of urgency assumes mammoth proportions until it submerges you. You then want the quickest route to get to where you want to be. Stop and catch your breath. Be still and know that He is God…and He cares.

OCTOBER 16

❧

However, as it is written: "What no eye has seen, what no ear has heard, and what no human mind has conceived"—the things God has prepared for those who love him—

1 CORINTHIANS 2:9

So, you decide to go off the beaten track and take the path less travelled. You travel through the woods, where the path dips sharply down and then goes steeply up again. You're seeing birds you have never seen before, and trees and shrubbery that make you marvel at the diversity of God's creation. You find wildflowers that you pick, to press between the pages of a book as a memory of this little adventure. And then, just when you thought you'd seen it all, you suddenly break out of the woods and see, spread out before you, a panoramic lake with crystal clear water and lilies growing by the bank. And that's just one of the many things that the Lord surprises you with at the end of a long trek through challenging territory. So, keep going girl, you're doing great, and there are blessings coming your way!

OCTOBER 17

❧

*...and you are of Christ, and
Christ is of God.*

1 CORINTHIANS 3:23

Oh the bliss of finding yourself. You're going to be doing that a few times through your life, though, especially if you are prone to losing yourself—whether in your work, studies, social circle or extra curricular activities. Every once in a while, it helps when somebody reminds you who you are. But it's an even greater help if you would stand in front of the mirror everyday and reinforce the truth that you are more than you think you are…and that you are evolving everyday. Remember you were created in the very image of God, so don't doubt your abilities, or the strength of your character and personality. Never be assailed by doubt about who you are in Christ, but be inspired by that truth every day.

OCTOBER 18

❦

*In him we were also chosen, having
been predestined according to the plan
of Him who works out everything in
conformity with the purpose of His will.*

EPHESIANS 1:11

You raised your hand and they didn't choose you. They didn't say yes, when you volunteered. You offered, but they refused. Shrug and walk away. They're not important. Neither are their schemes. But, on the other hand, you were *chosen*. It's a significant word. Hand selected. Singled out. Called. Preferred. *Chosen*—that's you! Chosen to succeed. Chosen to stand out. Chosen to rise up. Chosen to speak out. By the Lord! What a privilege! You know what's even more amazing? That you were *predestined* to do certain things and to assume certain roles. So don't hold back. Step into who you were predestined to be. Reach for what you were meant to accomplish. Woman, you're a wonder that was created to bring about transformation.

OCTOBER 19

*I keep asking that the God of our Lord
Jesus Christ, the glorious Father, may give
you the Spirit of wisdom and revelation,
so that you may know him better.*

EPHESIANS 1:17

Remember all those meals, lovingly prepared, that your mom or grandmom served you? And that car that your dad bought you? Or do you recall the many fun things that your parents plan, and do, with you? Picnics and games, movie nights and fishing trips? Have you considered that all these beautiful gestures find their root in God's loving heart? Today, mirror His love by doing something special for somebody. You will, in the process, find the Father's heart revealed to you and through you. Don't pass up an opportunity to take one more step towards self discovery and personal growth in wisdom, love and inspiration.

OCTOBER 20

I pray that the eyes of your heart may be enlightened in order that you may know the hope to which he has called you, the riches of his glorious inheritance in his holy people, and his incomparably great power for us who believe.

EPHESIANS 1:18-19

Martin Luther King Jr. said, *'We must accept finite disappointment, but never lose infinite hope.'* Your outlook on life forms the essence of who you are. People may scorn your perpetual sense of hope and optimism, but don't let their cynical attitude rain on your parade. You keep smiling, keep hoping and keep believing. Positive things are attracted to positive minded people. Good things will come to you when you hope. Doubt never has too much company, but belief has lots of friends. The two closest friends of belief are faith and hope. Hold fast to these and make them your constant companions. You will then prevail over the impossible.

OCTOBER 21

～

For it is by grace you have been
saved, through faith—and this is not
from yourselves, it is the gift of God...

EPHESIANS 2:8

One day you're down and out, and the next day you have been lifted up, out of the mire, and given a place where you feel safe and secure. You did nothing to deserve it. You just simply believed that the negative situation that you were in, was never going to be permanent. You believed, also, that God's promise that you were chosen for bigger and better things was about to come true. Because there's always a medal or a prize at the end of a gruelling race. And also because you know that your Father God never says anything that's not true. So, if He said you were blessed and fortunate, then it is true. He is a loving Father, and loves to give good gifts to his kids. Today, reach you and receive His free gift of grace which covers you in forgiveness and raises you up to salvation.

OCTOBER 22

I ask you, therefore, not to be discouraged...

EPHESIANS 3:13

The sun sets and rises again. The tide pulls back and swells once more. To every end there is another beginning. Life, like the air around you, is in a continuous state of movement. Nothing remains the same. There is only one constant, and that is God. Like the sun, He never moves away. He is right there, at the center of it all, shedding His radiant light on every dark situation, and bestowing warmth where the cold has crept into tired bones. Let this momentary slump be the slingshot that propels you to a new level of achievement. Use failure like a stepping-stone to success. If you don't believe in yourself, believe in God who dwells within you and renews your strength every day; giving you fresh hope and perspective. Bask in the light of His encouragement and soar ever higher.

OCTOBER 23

❧

As a prisoner for the Lord, then,
I urge you to live a life worthy of
the calling you have received.

EPHESIANS 4:1

From this moment on, dear beautiful girl, live the life of the princess that you are. Don't sell yourself short, and don't expect anything less than what you were promised. You were born to shine, so don't hide your light under a bushel. You may once have felt that you weren't special, and you allowed your assessment of yourself to shape your way forward. Now you know better. You have to look at yourself through the indulgent, loving eyes of your Heavenly Daddy who loves you so much and rejoices over you every day. If you're feeling a rush of joy and your spirits begin to soar as you read this, know that He is in every word here, because He knows that this is true and that it comes from Him.

OCTOBER 24

❧

You were taught, with regard to your former way of life, to put off your old self, which is being corrupted by its deceitful desires.

Barack Obama said, '*Change will not come if we wait for some other person or some other time. We are the ones we've been waiting for. We are the change that we seek.*' If you're waiting for your circumstances to change, think again. They can't, and won't, until you take charge. If you want something to change, you've got to make it happen. That's what makes you a game changer. Welcome change and yearn for transformation, but above all, pray for strength to be the change that you need. Today, dig deep, and look within yourself. Find out if you've become complacent. Question your efforts to go out there and make change happen. You're going to do amazing things with your life!

OCTOBER 25

❧

*Be kind and compassionate to one
another, forgiving each other...*

EPHESIANS 4:32

Nature is such an incredible example of forgiveness and patience. Take the forests, rivers and lakes—they put up with man's abuse and still keep giving and providing. Look at the animals—for the manner in which they have been hunted, they ought to be planning a widespread war, but they seem to forget what man has done, and they just keep delighting human eyes with their uniqueness and beauty. Think of a gazelle for instance, her limpid eyes, appealing for justice, yet none is given. Yet she forgives. You are of God, and God created nature. Therefore, you mirror the attributes of nature—her beauty, diversity, constancy and forgiveness. Today, let the hurt that people have inflicted, be thrust far away from you as you choose to forgive.

OCTOBER 26

For you were once darkness, but
now you are light in the Lord.
Live as children of light.

EPHESIANS 5:8

If you are wondering how people perceive you, or if they will welcome you with a smile, should you pay them a visit, remember that you are the ray of light that will brighten up their day. You can't escape that fact, girl. So, go out there and shine. Illuminate somebody's world with your smile. Also, that grudge you were holding? Perhaps it's time to let it go. It's been bowing you down as it gets heavier with each passing day, and that's not good for your posture! You need to hold yourself erect, and grudges and grouses don't help. Wear a bright colour today. Be joyful in your heart and know just how favoured you are. God is smiling down on His daughter and cheering you on.

OCTOBER 27

A good name is better than fine perfume.

ECCLESIASTES 7:1

Which girl doesn't love a good fragrance to spray on? For some, your perfume becomes your signature. You spend a lot on it, and you wear it with pride, because it's exclusive and expensive. You invest so much in this fragile bottle with its designer label. You invest your money, and you invest your time in selecting the perfect fragrance. Pretty soon, your friends associate the brand with you. So, even as you are thinking about that perfume, remember that even the finest fragrance can't disguise an unclean body or soul. Take special care to ensure the health of your soul and spirit, because that will define your character, and your character will define your reputation… and your reputation is something that sticks like glue. It's like the perfume. The smell lingers. It becomes associated with you. Let the fragrance of your soul reflect the light of heaven.

OCTOBER 28

❧

I saw that wisdom is better than folly,
just as light is better than darkness.

ECCLESIASTES 2:13

Everybody makes mistakes. No human being is infallible. But don't beat yourself up over it. Reflect on it, learn from it, and then move on. Even the truly wise once made mistakes, and used them as stepping-stones to wisdom. Wisdom is learned and not unattainable. Seek it every day. Woman, you have good instincts, which are invaluable in the pursuit of wisdom. And as you learn, impart your wisdom to others. The more you give, the more you receive, and the more your storehouse will be filled. So, emerge from your self-imposed exile, and come into the light of realisation. This is how it works. The palaces of the wise are built on a foundation of lessons learned through a series of mistakes. Don't forget, even great inventions went through a process of trial and error before they were perfected.

OCTOBER 29

⁓

The wise have eyes in their heads, while
the fool walks in the darkness…

ECCLESIASTES 2:14

You knew you shouldn't have gone there, done that, said this or thought that. But you did. You made a choice and that decision was made in your head. Your heart cringed at the decision, but your head said go ahead…or maybe it was the other way around. Girl, here's the deal. To begin to make better decisions, you have to be wise. To be wise you need to be in constant communication with the Voice of Wisdom. Begin a dialogue with Him today. He is God—the Lord of the Universe. By His grace you are set free from the consequences of your hasty actions. He wipes the slate clean and gives you another chance, as long as you make a decision not to go that route again. The fact is, you have a clean slate and a new day with a fresh start. So girl, no more self-condemnation. Stay positive.

OCTOBER 30

*There is a time for everything,
and a season for every activity
under the heavens.*

ECCLESIASTES 3:1

Patience is a virtue, and at your age you might be impatient to get to where you want to be. But the road of life is littered with the tattered remains of hasty decisions, so girl, hang in there. Wait for the right time. You will be rewarded for your patience. Whether it's waiting for the right partner, the right job or the right college course—just be patient. It will come to you in God's good time. He has a plan and believe me, it is an elaborate one. He has scheduled every day of your life and even built in a contingency plan for when you deviate from His Will. If you want to get to your goals faster, wait, be still. Be hasty and you risk delays. Always be assured that God has not taken His eye off you. You are a vital part of His plan. He is getting you to where you need to be, and He is shaping you in the process.

OCTOBER 31

❦

*Who is like the wise? Who knows
the explanation of things? A person's
wisdom brightens their face and
changes its hard appearance.*

ECCLESIASTES 8:1

Have you been losing sleep because you're worried? Or
have you been allowing your social life or studies to cut
into your hours of sleep? Well then, you're going to risk losing
that healthy glow. Your brain needs to rest and rejuvenate.
So does the rest of your body. You need stillness in order for
all your batteries to be recharged. It has also been proved
that you operate at peak when you are well rested. You make
better decisions, and definitely wiser ones. You become even
tempered and of a happier, lighter disposition. You glow with
an inner light, which is reflected in your face. Your eyes are
brighter, because the eyes, they say, are the windows of the
soul. And your soul has been revived and refreshed while you
slept. So basically, getting adequate hours of sleep are saving
you a small fortune on medical bills, beauty treatment and
lessons on wisdom. Not a bad deal, right?

NOTES

NOVEMBER

NOVEMBER 1

*Do not be carried away by all kinds
of strange teachings. It is good for our
hearts to be strengthened by grace…*

HEBREWS 13:9

People have an opinion on everything. It's up to you to be discerning and to develop insights into how best you can filter out what you need to, and retain whatever might be beneficial. However, be aware that the God is the ultimate authority on everything, and you need look no further than His Word for instruction and insight. He is well pleased with everyone who eagerly seeks His guidance. Girl, be wise. Exercise caution when it comes to things that assault your senses. Sweet words often conceal a devious tongue. Protect yourself with the strength that comes from deep within you.

NOVEMBER 2

~

*Consider it pure joy, my brothers and
sisters, whenever you face trials of many
kinds, because you know that the testing
of your faith produces perseverance.*

JAMES 1:2-3

Tests and trials are a regular part of life. They keep you
from becoming complacent and constantly prompt you
to exercise your faith. You learn courage under fire and how
to keep going despite the odds. At the end of every trial lies
a reward of joy. You are stronger and more resilient, and you
know how to take the next dip in the road. Fortitude and
foresight define your nature and cause people to regard you
with new respect. Continue to be humble, yet exult in the
strong, courageous woman that you are evolving into. Give
someone else a word of praise and approval. Share your joy
by lightening somebody else's load with a smile that says,
'keep going. You're getting there.'

NOVEMBER 3

❧

With this in mind, we constantly pray for you, that our God may make you worthy of His calling, and that by His power He may bring to fruition your every desire for goodness and your every deed prompted by faith.

2 Thessalonians 1:11

If you're wondering how you will take up a position of responsibility, change your self-doubt to self-belief. Your role on this planet was defined long ago. You just have to step into it. You are already equipped, simply by virtue of being who you are and doing what you were meant to. The rest falls into place. Just have faith that what has begun within you will reach maturity by the lessons that life is constantly teaching you. Have faith. Without faith you cannot understand or accept how perfectly you were created and shaped to fulfill the responsibilties that you are called upon to fulfill.

NOVEMBER 4

~

Don't let anyone deceive you in any way.

2 THESSALONIANS 2:3

Sometimes, because of your innocence and trusting nature, you might lay yourself open to deception. It's like leaving something valuable out on a park bench and running off to play with your dog. There are always prowlers about, waiting to steal something from you. Whether it's your peace, your trust or your belongings. Vigilance is key to survival. Watch your back while unlocking your front door. Literally and figuratively. Treat your heart like your front door and protect it from deceivers. Don't allow yourself to slip and fall on the words that slide off a smooth tongue. Take care, beautiful lady, life may not be an eternal 'non-slip' floor, but treading warily always helps.

NOVEMBER 5

⌒

May the Lord direct your hearts into
God's love and Christ's perseverance.

2 THESSALONIANS 3:5

Whatever you do out of love, or with a sense of love, motivates you to persevere. It's like the time your mom was sick and sent you to visit your grandmother in her place and take care of her for a week. It wasn't the easiest thing to do—because even loving grandmas get crotchety and talk endlessly. But you did what you did, out of a sense of duty born from love. You persevered. Base your choice of career on love too. It's something you have to stick with, so there's no point taking on something that you're only lukewarm about. Truly love and enjoy what you are doing and you will succeed because you persevere.

NOVEMBER 6

And as for you, brothers and sisters,
never tire of doing what is good.

2 THESSALONIANS 3:13

But nobody notices, you say. *I'm being taken for granted,* you cry. Maybe so, but you have to persist no matter what. Do what you're doing for the good of all, whether people are aware of it or not. Because it doesn't matter if they notice your efforts or applaud them. All that matters, is that you do the right thing because your Heavenly Daddy asks for nothing less, and He takes note and is well pleased with you. So, keep being the change that is required. Keep being the voice that speaks out. Keeping being the hands that serve. Give and it will be given to you.

NOVEMBER 7

～

Now may the Lord of peace himself give you peace at all times and in every way. The Lord be with all of you.

2 THESSALONIANS 3:16

Today don't run, walk. Take your earphones off. Don't track your miles. Just walk—in the park, maybe, where you hear and see life. Feel the pulse of this life. Watch the dogs romp with their owners. Feed the geese, or pigeons, or ducks. Take your shoes off and feel the earth beneath your feet. Wriggle your toes in the grass. Catch a butterfly on your palm and observe its wings pulsate. Admire its brilliant hues. Stroke the petals of a flower. Close your eyes and lay back on the grass and feel the sunlight filter through your eyelids. Breathe. Luxuriate in the tranquility of the moment. This life you have is a gift. Enjoy it!

NOVEMBER 8

❧

For what is our hope, our joy, or the crown in which we will glory in the presence of our Lord Jesus when He comes? Is it not you?

1 THESSALONIANS 2:19

Dear beautiful girl, today, as you look in the mirror, remind yourself of some vital truths. You are somebody's hope and someone else's joy. You are a significant part of someone's story. It's important that you never forget that, so that you understand that you were never meant to hold on to this life for yourself and yourself alone. You were meant to share it and to let people into it. Sadly, the only sharing most people do is on social media. When was the last time that you shared even a few kind words with someone who so desperately needed them? Today be someone's ray of sunshine. Bring donuts and coffee to someone who would never have expected such a kind gesture. How pleasantly surprised they will be. You're so special, girl. Go ahead and let some of that 'special' flow onto someone else.

NOVEMBER 9

~

*May he strengthen your hearts so that
you will be blameless and holy in the
presence of our God and Father when our
Lord Jesus comes with all his holy ones.*

1 Thessalonians 3:13

That pristine valley with the stream flowing gently through. That's you—with the spirit of kindness and gentleness running through you. That glorious blue sky—that protective canopy that yields sun and rain…that's you! Protector, nurturer, giver of warmth and provision. That exquisite ocean, teeming with life, adorned with a necklace of gold. That's you! So beautiful, bountiful. A reflection of God's goodness. That brook that seems to laugh through the ups and downs of the course it follows. That's you. Forever joyful; resilient despite the course of your life. Today, dear woman, celebrate your many facets. You are a force of energy. You are wisdom and you are the rain of good fortune.

NOVEMBER 10

❧

You are all children of the light and children of the day. We do not belong to the night or to the darkness.

1 THESSALONIANS 5:5

Adaptability—it's a word that drives home the need of the hour. Life is fluid. Circumstances change. The more adaptable you are, the happier you will be. If your parents announce a family vacation that you don't particularly want to go on, adapt. Comply. It will avoid unnecessary conflict. If you are asked to take a different class or work on a project with a team you don't choose, adapt. It's the biggest favour you can do yourself. Adaptible people are happy wherever they are. You never need to be a fish out of water, if you can go with the flow. It's all in your mind anyway. The only thing you should never comply with are situations that you know instinctively to be wrong.

NOVEMBER 11

Encourage the disheartened, help the weak, be patient with everyone. Make sure that nobody pays back wrong for wrong, but always strive to do what is good for each other and for everyone else.

1 THESSALONIANS 5:14-15

Revenge doesn't become a woman of strength and courage. It's never the best recourse. If someone hurts you, don't offend them in return. Just be good to them. Show them you're the bigger person. People often hurt others because they are hurting. They lash out because they don't know how to express, or deal with, their pain. Be patient. Keep being kind. If even kindness fails to change a person's attitude, then walk away. Don't lash out. Just gracefully exit and keep the person at a distance. You will reap the benefits of not stooping to a mode of behaviour that just isn't you, and of taking the high ground.

NOVEMBER 12

May God himself, the God of peace, sanctify you through and through. May your whole spirit, soul and body be kept blameless at the coming of our Lord Jesus Christ.

1 THESSALONIANS 5:23

There's peace in working with your hands. It rests your mind and strengthens your body. Today, consider taking a length of fine white linen and embroidering on it. Fill it with beautiful flowers. If you can't embroider, learn how. Teaching yourself new things promotes dexterity and keeps your brain young. Keeping your hands occupied by making something beautiful also promotes a sense of accomplishment. It also keeps you away from unnessarily getting dragged into issues and pursuits that only eat into valuable time and leave you angry and frustrated. When you engage your hands, your brain is happy and healthy. You feel good because you are using one of your many gifts.

NOVEMBER 13

❧

*But you, Lord, do not be far from
me. You are my strength; come
quickly to help me.*

PSALM 22:19

Sickness of the body is something we all have to deal with.
Sickness of the mind is something that somebody may
actually be suffering from, but are not aware of. Depression
due to loneliness is becoming more common now, as the
Internet is being more widely chosen as a substitute for
human contact. How long will people stare at their computer
or phone screens before realising they are actually suffering
from a malady that is killing them? Don't stay by yourself
today, but seek company. Be the visitor that someone is
praying will knock on their door. Virtual hugs keep doing
the rounds, devoid of warmth. Don't let an emoji take your
place in somebody's life.

NOVEMBER 14

❧

In you, Lord my God, I put my trust.

PSALM 25:1

When the sounds of the social or corporate jungle grow louder and more menacing; when there is more conflict than peace; when it seems like a disturbing situation is overwhelming you…take a walk or take a nap. When you sleep, answers come through your dreams. When you walk, your brain is refreshed by a flood of oxygen, and you get greater clarity. But even better is when you pray. Down on your knees, as you cry out to God and entrust a situation to Him, you are delivered from worry and anxiety. Walk away from conflict with a smile. Find your peace today. You owe it to yourself.

NOVEMBER 15

❧

No one who hopes in you will
ever be put to shame.

PSALM 25:3

Hope is seeing a hard, white cloud and believing it will rain on the parched earth below. Hope is looking into the face of a negative situation and finding something left to hold on to. Hope is a plank of wood on a rough sea when the ship has succumbed to the strength of the waves. Hope is a cluster of fireflies on a dark night, lighting up the gloom. Hold on to hope even if you hold on to nothing else. Hope is your lifeline and your life breath. If you lose hope, you lose it all. Hope is the foundation for tomorrow. Build on hope and you will build high.

NOVEMBER 16

❧

Show me your ways, Lord,
teach me your paths.

PSALM 25:4

Finding the right teacher or mentor is often quite difficult. You have to take what you get and even the best isn't good enough. The human mind is eager and hugry for information. Check the news and knowledge channels to know just how many people invest in information. Yet the best, most authentic knowledge comes to you from your one and only life source—your Maker and Creator. Learn from His Word. The news and knowledge channels on television can give you a surface view of what's going on and what happened once upon a time. But to get beneath the surface and reach the truth, come to Him… because all wisdom comes from Him.

NOVEMBER 17

❧

Guide me in your truth and teach
me, for you are God my Savior, and
my hope is in you all day long.

PSALM 25:5

So, she said this thing to you that she had heard from someone, who heard it from somebody else. You wonder if you should hold on to this snippet or pass it on, because to keep it to yourself would be selfish. Or would it? This is like a game of Chinese Whispers, and the news probably got twisted out of shape along the way. The message was tampered with, added to or deleted from, and now that you have it, you have an ethical duty—to add your dramatic bit and pass it on, or stomp out the rumour by breaking the chain. Ponder what you have heard. If it's no good to anybody and might be of some harm to somebody, let it go. Bury it and walk away. Truth is valuable. It never comes in the form of a rumour. It is delivered in the purest way—through a Voice you can trust. Search for the only true, authentic Truth today, by emptying your mind of all futile thoughts and leaving space only for what is important.

NOVEMBER 18

◈

My eyes are ever on the Lord, for only
he will release my feet from the snare.

PSALM 25:15

Oh, that was some mess you got yourself into. Circles of friends can sometimes get to be hotbeds of controversy. Words can trip you up like traps and snares that are deliberately laid out to catch you unawares. But now you're free, girl, don't go that route again. You made a mistake and you were rescued from the consequences. The lesson to be learned is to choose one's friends carefully. Be at peace with everyone but trust only the ones closest to you. Eventually everyone, even your dearest friend, could potentially let you down. The only One you can trust is The Lord, who will never leave you nor forsake you. He watches over you, and if you should ever get caught in a trap or a snare, He will be there to rescue you.

NOVEMBER 19

❧

Who, then, are those who fear the Lord?
He will instruct them in the ways they
should choose. They will spend
their days in prosperity, and their
descendants will inherit the land.

PSALM 25:12-13

Y ou have a roadmap for success. You have a route to prosperity. You can rise above every challenge and make it to your goals if you would only listen to the voice of wisdom. And it is said that to get wisdom, you must begin with fear of The Lord. Fear is not to hide and tremble. Fear is respect for His authority and an awareness that if you do not follow the path He gives you, you aren't going to get very far. If you want to go places, have a great career, and really step into the fullness of who you are, then listen to what the Lord has to say and follow His Will.

NOVEMBER 20

The Lord confides in those who fear him;
he makes his covenant known to them.

PSALM 25:14

Promises are so special. You almost wish that the people who make them, would respect and keep them. Have a simple rule not to disappoint anyone—if you can't keep a promise, don't make it. Vows are even more sacred—sealed with rings to make an even greater impact. People seem to mean them when they make them, but forget them and break them. This is the reality, but you can change it. Before making a promise or taking a vow, think very deeply about it. Don't take them lightly. They will impact your future and someone else's. Choose your words carefully before you speak. Let wisdom guide your tongue.

NOVEMBER 21

❧

Turn to me and be gracious to me, for I am lonely and afflicted. Relieve the troubles of my heart and free me from my anguish.

PSALM 25:16-17

It's a sad truth that all to often when you are afflicted, people tend to leave you alone. They don't know how to cope with your predicament. They have little or no helpful advice to give. So you battle it out on your own, and you learn a valuable lesson in the process—that nobody should be left alone when they are in the state that you have been in. Then you go out of your way to reach into the loneliness of someone else's life and provide relief. You've been there, so you know a little bit about what they're going through, even though you understand that each one has their own story to tell and their own experience of grief or affliction. Keep doing what you're doing. You are bringing healing into a life, and hope for another day.

NOVEMBER 22

~

May integrity and uprightness protect me,
because my hope, Lord, is in you.

PSALM 25:21

C.S. Lewis said, '*Integrity is doing the right thing, even when no one is watching*'. It's what makes you who you are and sets you apart as someone who can be trusted. Integrity is makes for harmony and understanding. There is peace to be found in the presence of Integrity. Integrity doesn't steal or lie or let someone down. It's almost akin to love. Love is Integrity with a heart around it. Hold Integrity close to your heart. Let it become a vital part of who you are and what you are known for. Fame and fortune evaporate in a lifetime, but Integrity is celebrated for eternity. Choose Integrity above other attributes. Let it be the hallmark of your character. From Integrity come other values like honesty and generosity. Girl, in all your dealings with people let there be Integrity. And let there be Uprightness. Let them hold you up like bookends. Let them walk on either side of you through the darkest stretches of the road.

NOVEMBER 23

❧

*For I have always been mindful of
your unfailing love and have lived in
reliance on your faithfulness*

PSALM 26:3.

The bird rises at dawn, while it is still dark, and knows
that it will find food. All night it has roosted in a secure
branch of a tree. Its nest didn't fall when the wind blew. It
knows that there will be provision for its young. And that at
the height of the sun, there will be shade and water to drink.
It flies high and free. It has no cares or anxieties. How much
that bird could teach you. How to trust that your needs will
be met and that you will want for nothing because you have
the promise of God that His protection ensures that you are
provided for.

NOVEMBER 24

❧

To you, Lord, I call; you are my Rock.

PSALM 28:1

Could you think of anything better than a cool rock to sit on, on a beautiful sunny day, white you enjoy an ice cream cone or a pensive hour of fishing? There's something so comforting about a rock. It's constant, ageless, eternal. It can never be moved, and even when you revisit it decades later, it's still there. Maybe you're one of the people who carved your initials in a rock face for posterity. Or maybe you buried a time capsule at the base of a rock—knowing it would be easy to find years later. That's why The Lord is so often referred to as our Rock. Because He is always there, and ever dependable. Today, be a rock to someone. Let somebody lean on you. Be the person they can trust and rely on.

NOVEMBER 25

The Lord is my strength and my shield;
my heart trusts in him, and he helps me.
My heart leaps for joy, and with
my song I praise him.

PSALM 28:7

Remember the rock? Well, it's a strong shield from harsh weather. You can shelter by a rock when it rains or when a storm comes. Houses built on rocks stand firm—literally and figuratively. You can trust the strength and reliability of a rock. It will never let you down. It will hold you up and keep you safe when the flood waters rise. You have something of the rock inside of you. It's determination and resilience. People rely on you. They know that you will always be there for them. Especially when times are hard. That's who you are, woman. A rock. Just like The Lord is your rock.

NOVEMBER 26

❧

*I will exalt you, Lord, for you
lifted me out of the depths.*

PSALM 30:1

When you feel yourself in over your head, don't panic. So you went too far away from the relative safety of your comfort zone and you found it difficult to navigate the deep. Don't worry, girl, you're going to be fine. His eye is on you. He sees your struggle and comes to your rescue. He quietens the storm. He makes the flood waters abate. He lifts you up and sets you on a rock. He takes your hand and tells you that its alright. Whatever the situation that you found yourself in, He lifts you high above it. You know that you can count on Him. He will come through for you every time. And you have become wiser for the experience.

NOVEMBER 27

❧

*Praise be to the Lord, for he showed
me the wonders of his love.*

PSALM 31:21

Forgiveness is liberating. Both to forgive and to be forgiven. It's like being freed from a pair of very restrictive shackles. It's hard to forgive and it's equally difficult for someone else to forgive you. But once you have broken through the barriers it's like you're able to breathe again. The weight on your shoulders is lifted. The restraints that seemed to choke the very breath out of your lungs is gone forever. You feel lighter, freer, healthier. Today forgive yourself too. Let yourself off the hook for transgressions that are real or imagined. You have been forgiven by The Lord and you need to allow that forgiveness to liberate you once and for all. When you forgive yourself, it's also easier to forgive others.

NOVEMBER 28

～

*For I know that through your prayers and
God's provision of the Spirit of Jesus
Christ what has happened to me
will turn out for my deliverance.*

PHILIPPIANS 1:19

There's an old country song by Garth Brooks that goes,
'Some of God's greatest gifts are unanswered prayers.' There
may be times when you feel like everything is going wrong.
There seems to be no way out. You pray and the situation just
gets worse. You wonder what you did to deserve it because
you have been doing everything right and then this happens.
Cheer up girl, things are actually working out just fine.
God always uses some of the direst circumstances to work
His Will. He can turn some of your worst experiences into
blessings. And one day you will look back at something you
wanted but didn't get, no matter how loud you cried out to
the heavens…and you'll know, that was a blessing. He knows
what you need. He knows what's best for you.

NOVEMBER 29

◦~◦

*For it is God who works in you to will and
to act in order to fulfill his good purpose.*

PHILIPPIANS 2:13

If you feel like you're drifting through life, remember this is just a phase. You will figure it out. You will understand your role in the grand scheme of things. You are not just a cog in the wheel, but an integral and important part of God's plan. He called you lovingly into this world and He has a future laid out for you—like a beautiful landscape—with every minute detail worked out. So no, you're not drifting. It might feel like it, but you are on a trajectory. You're just finding your way to your path. Sometimes you may stumble about in the dark, and at other times it will feel like you have it all figured out. Girl, you have your story. It's only just beginning. Be patient. Give it time.

NOVEMBER 30

❧

*Many, Lord my God, are the wonders you
have done, the things you planned for us.
None can compare with you;*

When the sky is filled with stars and the world sleeps.
When the moon, like a beacon of hope shines above
you… take the time to look up and praise God for the beauty
of the moment. Perhaps you have taken nature for granted
recently. Maybe you tell yourself that there'll be other star
filled nights and full moons to admire. But not this one. Not
this hour. Savour every precious minute you have here on
this earth. Make it count. Each moment is a gift, and each
gift is unique. Each starlit evening, and every moonlit night
is different from the other. Because they are set in different
moments in time. Take this bounty, freely given, and use it
well. Be inspired by it. Be awed by it. Be grateful for it.

NOTES

DECEMBER

DECEMBER 1

~

But I am like a green olive tree in the house of God. I trust in the steadfast love of God forever and ever.

Well, here we are in the season of Advent and looking forward to the Christmas. There is probably no happier season than the holiday season. And every day is bright with hope and joy. What will you be doing today? How will you be spending the rest of the week? Girl, today, think of someone you can bring some joy to. Volunteer in a soup kitchen or decorate a homeless shelter. Bring a Christmas tree across to somebody who can't afford one. Be someone's secret Santa. This is the time to be loving and giving. And plan to make some of your Christmas gifts. There's nothing better than gifting someone the work of your hands.

DECEMBER 2

❦

O God, hear my prayer; give ear
to the words of my mouth.

PSALM 54:2

Hmmm… day two of Advent and it's time for a mug of hot chocolate with marshmallows floating on the top. It's also time to celebrate warmth and good cheer, so light a fire in the grate and settle down in front of it. You've worked hard through the year and it's time to soak in the spirit of Christmas. Make a flask of hot chocolate and carry it with you on your walk, along with some disposable cups. Give a homeless person a steaming cup of your hot chocolate and share the Christmas spirit. Shop with caution. Don't overspend or pile up bills that you might not be able to pay. Remember it's okay not to shop till you drop, even if everyone else is doing it.

DECEMBER 3

~

Behold, God is my helper; the Lord
is the upholder of my life.

PSALM 54:4

Day three of Advent. The streets are so pretty. The shops are all lit up. There's such a feeling of joyous anticipation in the air. Go out and enjoy it. Remember how every Christmas tree carries a special message—the evergreen branches are symbolic of the eternal life Jesus gives to everyone who believes in Him. What a happy thought. Share the message with someone. Give a homeless person a meal, and maybe take some toys and gifts to an orphanage. When you give joy you receive a double portion of it in return. Give without counting the cost. Call a friend that you haven't been in touch with and make her day. If she lives close enough, pay her a visit and give her something that you made yourself.

DECEMBER 4

For he has delivered me from every trouble.

PSALM 54:7

The fourth day of Advent. If you haven't put your decorations up, then this would be a good time to do so. Clear out a closet and put things you aren't using into boxes. Add clothes and shoes you haven't worn in a year to the pile. Take the boxes across to a homeless shelter or an orphanage, or any place where these items will be put to good use. You can make someone's day just by sharing what you have. There are people who don't have warm clothes this winter. You do your bit to outfit some of them with coats and sweaters that you haven't worn in a while but are still in excellent condition. You will feel on top of the world!

DECEMBER 5

∽

When I am afraid,
I put my trust in you.
In God, whose word I praise,
in God I trust; I shall not be afraid.

PSALM 56:3-4

The fifth day of Advent. Someone out there is missing out on the Christmas spirit because they are all alone. Trust God to lead you to them. Pack some ornaments and decorations in a box and take them out to a Senior Citizens' home. Take some board games as well, if you have them, and play games with the people there. You will be demonstrating the meaning of Christmas in the best way possible. Take time to listen to someone's problems. Let them pour out their hearts to you. Help them feel better with a few kind words and a hug. Involve your new friends at the Senior Citizens' home with putting up the ornaments and decorations you have brought them. You will be sharing joy and making precious memories!

DECEMBER 6

❧

For in you my soul takes refuge;
in the shadow of your wings
I will take refuge...

PSALM 57:1

Day six of Advent. Christmas is coming closer. Put your knitting skills to good use and knit some warm socks for people who can't afford to buy them. You can also knit some personalised Christmas stockings to gift to your loved ones. Today would be a good day to visit your grandparents, or an aunt or uncle, and help them clean or paint their homes or decorate their Christmas trees. Take them something you have made—like handpainted pinecones or a handmade wreath. Something simple, yet evocative of the Season. Remember, it's not the cost of the gift that matters, but the thought behind it. Make sure your gifts are meaningful.

DECEMBER 7

❧

I will give thanks to you, O Lord, among the peoples; I will sing praises to you among the nations. For your steadfast love is great to the heavens, your faithfulness to the clouds.

PSALM 57:9-10

Ah, the seventh day of Advent has arrived! There's excitement in the air. Join a group of Carol Singers or get your family together and go Carol Singing. Make sure to visit a homeless shelter or a home for the elderly, and bring them some joy with your singing. Bake some Christmas cookies and take them with you, to give to people who can't afford to make them or buy them. Get your friends and family involved in the project. You will enjoy the activity and bring joy to many people. If you've finished knitting those warm wollen socks, bring them along too.

DECEMBER 8

～

Praise be to the God and Father of our Lord Jesus Christ! In his great mercy he has given us new birth into a living hope through the resurrection of Jesus Christ from the dead, and into an inheritance that can never perish, spoil or fade. This inheritance is kept in heaven for you.

1 PETER 1:3-4

Day eight of Advent. What a wonderful day and what a blessed Season of hope. Today, plan to help your grandparents feel younger, able, and useful, by getting them involved in some holiday related activity. Maybe you could ask your grandmum to share her recipe for Gingerbread cookies with you. Then ask her to make them with you. Or ask granddad if he could help you with a DIY project. Spending time with your family is invaluable, particularly with the elderly. You are a source of joy to them. So give of your time unstintingly. Christmas gifts don't always have to be in the form of material things. They could just be about you giving of yourself and your time. You will receive more joy from doing this, than you ever would have imagined.

DECEMBER 9

❧

As obedient children, do not conform to the evil desires you had when you lived in ignorance. But just as he who called you is holy, so be holy in all you do; for it is written: "Be holy, because I am holy."

1 PETER 1:14-16

The ninth day of Advent. Get a recipe for homemade chocolates and make a batch of them. Fill pouches with them and tie them with pretty, colourful bows. Take them across to the friends you haven't met in a while. Maybe take some to friends you fell out with over a difference of opinion. This is the Season of forgiveness, so spread some of that around at this time. Forgiving somebody is like throwing off a weight that you have been carrying around needlessly. Besides, it's time to leave anger and bitterness behind. It's Christmas after all, and those twinkly lights everywhere remind you that you need to be like them—illuminating even the darkest of places.

DECEMBER 10

*Through these he has given us his very great
and precious promises, so that through
them you may participate in the divine
nature, having escaped the corruption
in the world caused by evil desires.*

2 PETER 1:4

Girl, it's day ten of Advent! We're getting closer to Christmas and the sense of anticipation is ramping up. Call on a neighbour who lives on her own and offer to help with her grocery shopping, or maybe suggest that you will drive her to the store so she has company. You could also offer to help her put up some decorations if she isn't feeling particularly inclined to do so, since she's on her own. Get her excited about the holidays. Share the Christmas spirit. Bake and frost cookies with her, and have a few laughs over cups of hot chocolate. Maybe you could even show her how she can make DIY Christmas cards or ornaments. It's so much better to give than to receive. Today, just give more of your time to others.

DECEMBER 11

◦❦◦

*For this very reason, make every effort
to add to your faith goodness; and to
goodness, knowledge; and to knowledge, self-
control; and to self-control, perseverance; and
to perseverance, godliness; and to godliness,
mutual affection; and to mutual affection, love.*

2 PETER 1:5-7

Day eleven of Advent, and you can almost hear those
sleighbells in the snow. Gather your family around
the fire for a good old-fashioned singsong, and make sure
you invite your grandparents as well. Tell your mum to put
her feet up while you cook dinner with your siblings. Make
some eggnog. Get everyone involved with baking Christmas
cake. Take a family photograph and send it out in an E-Card.
Make a video of everyone together and send it out to friends
and family who couldn't be with you at this time. Today,
shed grudges. Don't let sibling rivalry or any old feelings of
resentment cloud the day. Get rid of them once and for all.
What you don't hold onto, can't get a grip on you.

DECEMBER 12

~❧~

*Therefore, dear friends, since you have been
forewarned, be on your guard so that you
may not be carried away by the error of the
lawless and fall from your secure position.*

2 PETER 3:17

Hey girl, it's the twelvth day of Advent! Only a dozen days to go till Christmas Eve! What would you like to do today? How will you keep spreading the Christmas spirit? How about buying some candles and then decorating them to give away? Everyone loves candles. How much more candles that are adorned with sparkle and glitter. Wrap them up and take them across to people who make your life easier—your healthcare provider, dental hygienist or even the local fire station. Take some Christmas cake along too, or some gingerbread men or cookies. Let your gifts reflect the joy of the Season. Candles are so symbolic—they shed light in the darkness, like the birth of Christ did, two thousand years ago!

DECEMBER 13

⁕

*Be merciful to those who doubt; save
others by snatching them from
the fire;to others show mercy.*

JUDE 22-23

It's day thirteen of Advent. Aren't you excited? Or are you beginning to feel a little pressured by all that remains to be done before Christmas Day? Remember, Christmas is all about joy, and not stress, so eliminate all the stress points for both yourself and others. Tell someone about the true meaning of Christmas—of Jesus and His gift of forgiveness and eternal life—the beautiful message that we celebrate this Season. Accompany the story with something that you made to reflect the love and joy of Christmas. Maybe a hand made ornament, or a Christmas Cake that you baked and decorated yourself.

DECEMBER 14

❧

"I have loved you," says the Lord.

MALACHI 1:2

Day fourteen of Advent, and we're getting even closer to Christmas. There's so much love in the air that it's almost tangible. If you look back at the last thirteen days, you will see that you spread a lot of that love yourself, and that because you did, somebody else did too, and the chain continued. Today ponder on how that chain of love began two thousand years ago when a young woman was told she was going to have a baby and that He would save the world. What a blissful reason to be celebrating at this time. Volunteer at a children's shelter or an orphanage and play games with the kids. Build a snowman if it's snowing, or show the kids how to make snow angels. You be their snow angel!

DECEMBER 15

❧

The tongue of the wise adorns knowledge.

PROVERBS 15:2

Hey wise and wonderful woman, you've some such a long way. The year is almost out and it's Day Fifteen of Advent. There are Christmas trees wherever you look—in every store window and even on the sidewalk! There are lights everywhere, yet in some places there is darkness. Muster a team of volunteers and go out to those places. Maybe take food baskets or boxes of groceries to a neighbourhood where there are people who can't afford to celebrate Christmas. Leave the boxes on their porches for them to find. Surprise someone with your generosity today. When you take these gifts across to the people who desperately need them, maybe sing some Carols. Spread Christmas cheer.

DECEMBER 16

❦

The Lord works out everything
to its proper end.

PROVERBS 16:4

It's Day Sixteen of Advent. The first two weeks have gone by so fast! Time surely does fly when you're having fun! And isn't it great that instead of thinking of all the gifts people could give you, you are thinking of what you can give to people? So, what do you have planned for today? Don't you think holly is such an integral part of Christmas? Did you know that the prickly leaves are symbolic of the crown of thorns placed on Jesus's head, and the berries symbolised the blood that He shed? Today, get bunches of holly leaves and gift them to people at your school or place of work. Tell people what holly represents and why it's so special.

DECEMBER 17

~

The God of heaven will give us success.

Nehemiah 2:20

It's Day Seventeen and the air is filled with the sweet smell of cinnamon rolls. Do a practice run for when you make them on Christmas morning. Play some Christmas carols. Invite your neighbours to join in singing Carols in your backyard around a blazing bonfire. Toast marshmallows and serve eggnog. Get everyone involved with stoking the fire and serving the food. Perhaps you could have a barbecue. Getting together with the community is always important. Share the story of Christmas with someone who isn't familiar with it. Remind someone that the only gift worth giving is that of selfless love. Take a look at yourself in the mirror and celebrate how much you've grown as a person this past year.

DECEMBER 18

❧

The children of your servants will live
in your presence; their descendants will
be established before you.

PSALM 102:28

Christmas is so close! It's the Eighteenth Day of Advent.
Aim not to join the frenzied shoppers. Cut your list
down to the bare essentials—simple gifts and nothing more.
Don't get sucked into unnecessary expenditure and possible
debt. Be alert and wise. Your loved ones will be happy with
whatever you give them. They will most especially be grateful
for the time you spend with them. Take your mom out for a
movie and talk to her. Stop for a meal or coffee. Don't think
about school or work…or anything else during that time
with her. Give her your undivided attention and you will be
making a memory that you both will revisit for days to come.

DECEMBER 19

*For as high as the heavens are
above the earth, so great is his
love for those who fear him.*

Pssst! It's the Nineteenth Day of Advent! Five days till Christmas! Wrap your gifts for your loved ones and bake a few more batches of cookies to take to another homeless shelter. Call all your friends and relatives and tell them you'll be coming around to collect all the warm clothes they have no more use for. Enlist the help of some volunteers and then go out to collect the clothes and other things that your family and friends are giving away. Take them across to distribute at a shelter. Spend time helping to serve a meal and talk to the people there. You'll be amazed at the stories they have to tell. You'll be even more amazed at how their stories will change your perspective of life.

DECEMBER 20

᠆ঙ

As far as the east is from the west, so far
has he removed our transgressions from us.

PSALM 103:12

It's the Twentieth Day of Advent. The meaning of Christmas is becoming clearer—that God sent His son into the world as a gift, to forever erase the mistakes we have made and declare us free. Freedom is a wonderful feeling. Yet there are people out there who have never known what it's like to feel liberated from their past. Go out and find somebody to share this truth with, over a hot cup of coffee or cocoa. Christmas is not to be kept to yourself, but to be shared. Like the gifts you're getting ready to give to your friends and loved ones. So share the meaning and message of this occasion as well.

DECEMBER 21

❧

Remember me, Lord, when you show favor to your people, come to my aid when you save them.

PSALM 106:4

Yes, it's the Twenty first Day of Advent. Your tree is trimmed. The lights are winking on it. The decorations are up around the house and you're looking at the holly with a new realisation of what it symbolises. The holidays are a significant celebration of the birth of Him who died so you could live. If you have a sense of freedom today, it's because of this event two thousand years ago. Today, give something else away that's just lying around and not being used. How about all those beautifully illustrated books that brightened up your childhood? Think of how happy they would make a child who cannot afford to buy books like these. Pack them in a box and take them across to a children's home or shelter, and spend some time reading to the children and telling them stories.

DECEMBER 22

❧

He turned the desert into pools of water and
the parched ground into flowing springs;

PSALM 107:35

Day Twenty-two of Advent. You have probably woken up with a growing feeling of excitement. You can't help it. Christmas is like that. It just sends your spirits soaring. Gather your team of Carol Singers and do a round of your neighbourhood today. Take everyone in your family, including the kids. If you have Santa or Elf hats and ears, wear them. Be silly and don a pair of antlers or a red nose. It's the only time of year when you can be forgiven for sporting the craziest accessories. Enjoy the moment. Share it. Give someone on the street a Santa hat or a pair of antlers. The kids at the shelter will love them. Give them some joy too. Stop by and sing Carols with them and take some bags of marshmallows along to roast in the fire. Joy is infectious. It spreads. And it comes back to you in double measure.

DECEMBER 23

❦

With God we will gain the victory.

PSALM 108:13

D ay Twenty-Three of Advent. Lovely lady, you are such a source of light and life. Just look at how many lives you've touched over the past weeks. You have been amazing! Today, spend some time with your dad. Ask him to help you finish that DIY gift you're making for a friend or sibling. Urge him to tell you some stories from his childhood. Chat with him over cookies and cocoa. Moments like these are precious. Get everyone to cook a meal together. Assign tasks to each family member. Set the table and light some candles. Make it an occasion. Play a game over dinner. Make everyone recall a special Christmas memory. Write them down for posterity. Your heavenly daddy is smiling down on you as He sees how his little girl has grown into the confident, loving, giving young woman He intended her to be.

DECEMBER 24

❦

Therefore the Lord himself will
give you a sign. Behold, the virgin
shall conceive and bear a son, and
shall call his name Emmanuel.

ISAIAH 7:14

It's the Twenty Fourth Day of Advent! Christmas Eve is here. Arrange your presents under the tree. And remember those woollen stockings you were knitting? Fill them with fruit and chocolates and take them to the people who have no roof above their heads this cold winter. And then spend time with your family because it's important that you do. Attend a Christmas Eve Service with everyone and come back to a meal you all would have cooked together. Tomorrow is a big day with lots to get done. Begin some of the preparation today. But take time to sit outside on the porch and look up at the sky… and remember a star two thousand years ago that guided some shepherds and three Kings to visit Jesus where He lay in a manger in Bethlehem, wrapped in 'swaddling clothes'.

DECEMBER 25

～

For to us a child is born,
to us a son is given; and the government
shall be upon his shoulder, and his name
shall be called Wonderful Counselor, Mighty
God, Everlasting Father, Prince of Peace.

ISAIAH 9:6

Christmas Day! Joy to the World! Celebrate Jesus today. Celebrate the gift of love and peace. Prolong the time opening gifts together as a family. Savour each moment. Enjoy the meal you cook together. Make it special, not by spending a lot of money on it, but by spending time cooking it together. Invite people who don't have a family to celebrate with, and make sure there's something under the tree for them too. Have little containers handy to pack leftovers for everyone to take home. Play a game outdoors if the weather permits. Definitely play an indoor game, and get thoroughly immersed in it. Don't let the day go by without telling your family how much they mean to you. Maybe you could express those sentiments on handmade cards attached to your gifts.

DECEMBER 26

~c

Give, and it will be given to you. A good measure, pressed down, shaken together and running over, will be poured into your lap. For with the measure you use, it will be measured to you."

LUKE 6:38

Lovely Lady, you've done such a great job over Christmas. Today, relax and breathe. Think about what your faith means to you. Ponder this thought—that He came to save everyone, yet there are so many out there who think the Holidays are just about shopping and turkey. Maybe you could post the story of Christmas on your social media page, with photographs of what you have been doing through the Season. Encourage others to do likewise. Especially make people aware of how important Christmas really is. That if it wasn't for Christmas, we wouldn't have hope and life. Above all, know that love is better shown than talked of. Jesus spread love through the things He did. We know He loves us because He died so we could live. Continue to show your love through your kind deeds, throughout the year.

DECEMBER 27

~❧~

*The light shines in the darkness, and
the darkness has not overcome it.*

JOHN 1:5

The Christmas lights still twinkle everywhere, but there's a sense of the year drawing to a close, now that Christmas Day has come and gone. The snowfall reminds you of how Seasons change, and years come and go. Only one thing remains constant. The message and meaning of Christmas—that God loved the world so much that He gave us His only son, so that everyone who believes in Him will not die but live forever. Share this truth—it is the light that shines in an otherwise rapidly darkening world. The more you spread this light, the more the world is illuminated. Bring this truth to someone today and every day.

DECEMBER 28

~⁓~

He then added, "Very truly I tell you, you will see heaven open…"

JOHN 1:51

Girl, the year is almost done. But it's not over yet. Take the next few days to pray about how you will navigate the year to come. Lay out your plans and goals and ask God to direct your paths. Let Him tell you what you should do and where you should go. By ourselves we make choices that are limiting at best, but with Him we make choices that take us places we never ever imagined. Today, ask God to speak into your heart. Feel peace. He has great plans for everyone who abides by His Will. Talk to a friend and help them come to this realisation. Calm their fears for the future. Pray with them. Help them understand that with God they can do the impossible.

DECEMBER 29

~

Jesus replied, "Very truly I tell you, no one can see the kingdom of God unless they are born again."

JOHN 3:3

The simple truth is this—that with The Lord Jesus Christ, you can have a whole new life. So if you haven't already given all of your life to Him, maybe it's time to do so. Being born again simply means dying to your old self and coming alive in Him. It means letting go of past habits, hurt and grief. Girl, you have proved that you are a new creation in Him. You have evolved and transformed through the past months, and you are ready to go into the new year as a new person. Just ask Jesus to take charge. He just wants you to acknowlege Him as Lord of your life. It's a simple declaration that you make which gives you a brand new start. What better way to enter the New Year?

DECEMBER 30

For God so loved the world that he gave his one and only Son, that whoever believes in him shall not perish but have eternal life.

JOHN 3:16

It's the second last day of the year and maybe you're cleaning out your closet. Literally and figuratively. Maybe you're getting rid of everything that was unproductive and non-essential in your life. You go girl! You're a winner. You know that you want a new life and you are going all out to claim it. He has already given it to you. Celebrate it. While you're getting rid of things that you don't want to carry into the New Year, don't hold anything back. Give it all away. Give it all to Him. That relationship that went sour, that friend who hurt you, that course which didn't work out, and that job you didn't get. Let it all go and make place for all the new things that God is bringing into your life—new experiences, friendships and learning opportunities.

DECEMBER 31

❦

He who was seated on the throne said,
"I am making everything new!" Then
he said, "Write this down, for these
words are trustworthy and true."

REVELATION 21:5

He spoke and so shall it be. All things are new! When you enter the New Year, you go in as a *'new creation'*. Don't look back. Keep going forward. Tonight, choose to spend the last few hours and minutes of the year in prayer. Lift yourself and your family up to God and ask for His grace, so freely given. Take a walk and feel the peace that He surrounds you with. Exult in His presence. The old has gone and the new has come. Express your gratitude. Don't take the crossover from one year to the other lightly. Don't make lists with your resolutions, but instead ask God for guidance on how you should order your life in the New Year. He will tell you what to do and what not to. "In all your ways acknowledge Him, and He will direct your paths."

Happy New Year beautiful girl! Stay blessed!

NOTES

ABOUT THE AUTHOR

❧

G race McEwan is a pastor who thinks of herself as a servant before anything else. She lives for her congregation and sees her life's purpose as lifting them up.

It wasn't until late in life, after overcoming hardship with the help of God and answering the questions that had brought her doubt, that she decided to share some of her thoughts with a broader audience.

Bible Verses About Confidence is Grace's first book.